A W N Pugin

THE VICTORIAN SOCIETY

The Victorian Society is the champion for Victorian and Edwardian buildings in England and Wales. Our aims are:

CONSERVING

To save Victorian and Edwardian buildings of special architectural merit from needless destruction or disfigurement.

INVOLVING

To awaken appreciation of the best in Victorian and Edwardian architecture and the related arts.

EDUCATING

To encourage the study of Victorian and Edwardian buildings and also provide advice to owners and public authorities for their care and, where necessary, adaptation. Together these aims seek to increase the likelihood of conserving an essential part of Britain's heritage which is irreplaceable, cherished, diverse, beautiful, and part of everyday life.

Victorian and Edwardian buildings contribute greatly to the character of places which people love and where they live. They belong to all of us, since their owners are really only custodians for future generations.

When decisions are taken affecting their future, the debate must be open and informed. We need to understand what is special about them so that any changes can be incorporated without damaging them forever. We don't want to lose our past through ignorance.

The Victorian Society acts as a reservoir of expertise and energetic campaigners bringing together individuals from all round the country, and helps people to save the buildings they value. Sometimes it has been major national monuments such as the Albert Memorial in London or the Albert Dock in Liverpool, but more often nowadays it is local churches that are at risk from closure or damaging reordering, or perfectly good houses threatened by banal flat or office developments.

victoriansociety.org.uk

VICTORIAN ARCHITECTS

A W N Pugin

David Frazer Lewis

 Historic England

THE VICTORIAN SOCIETY
The champion for Victorian and Edwardian architecture

Published by Liverpool University Press on behalf of
Historic England, The Engine House, Fire Fly Avenue, Swindon SN2 2EH
www.HistoricEngland.org.uk

Historic England is a Government service championing England's heritage and giving expert,
constructive advice.

The views expressed in this book are those of the author and not necessarily those of
Historic England.

First published 2021

978-1-80034-864-6 paperback

British Library Cataloguing in Publication data
A CIP catalogue record for this book is available from the British Library.

For more information about images from the Archive, contact Archives Services Team,
Historic England, The Engine House, Fire Fly Avenue, Swindon SN2 2EH; telephone (01793) 414600.

Series editor: Andrew Saint

Page layout by Carnegie Book Production
Printed in the Czech Republic via Akcent Media Limited.

Front cover: Interior of St Giles', Cheadle. [Author]
Back cover: The only known photograph of A Welby Pugin. [Private Collection]

Contents

Acknowledgements

I was suddenly immersed in the world of Pugin studies in 2014, when I was appointed editor of the Pugin Society's peer-reviewed journal, *True Principles*. I would like to thank Catriona Blaker and Judith Al-Seffar for their early assistance, but most of all Joanna Lyall, who was exceedingly kind and kept me informed about society business. She made sure my views were relayed to the committee meetings, even after I moved back to the United States and had to oversee the publication remotely. Through the Pugin Society I was able to meet some of the greatest scholars of Pugin, who expanded my own understanding of the man and his work and brought me up to date with the latest scholarship. Alexandra Wedgwood's encouragement and gentle correction of popular misunderstandings about Pugin were very helpful. The late Dr Margaret Belcher of the University of Canterbury, New Zealand, was patient with the mistakes of a green editor and eventually entrusted me with the publication of some of the rare Pugin material she had gathered. Dr Timothy Brittain-Catlin, of the University of Kent, who has done as much as anyone living to promote Pugin studies, both by refining True Principles into a vessel for serious scholarship and by bringing an architect's eye to Pugin's house designs, gave me several hours of his time over multiple meetings to share insight into Pugin's world. Rosemary Hill, while a visiting fellow at All Soul's College, Oxford, helpfully allowed me to observe her lectures on the pre-Pugin phases of the Gothic Revival.

For the writing of this book, I would like to thank Michael Hall and Andrew Saint, who commissioned the book on behalf of the Victorian Society; John Hudson, who acted as my first editor at Historic England; and Alison Welsby, who became my editor when the series moved to Liverpool University Press. The Historians of British Art generously awarded me their annual publication grant to help cover the cost of illustrations. Gratitude is also due to the librarians and archivists who have assisted me at the RIBA, the V&A, the Bodleian, the YCBA, and many other institutions. Dr Richard Butler, of the University of Leicester, went out of his way to provide images of Pugin's works in Ireland. I would like to thank Dr Edward Gillin, then based at Cambridge, one of the sharpest of the new-vintage Victorianists, for sharing ideas about Victorian architecture and science and providing encouragement. Dr William Whyte and Dr Geoffrey Tyack of Oxford, who advised my doctoral thesis, laid the groundwork on which this book and my work for the Pugin Society were based. My appreciation of their continued support and willingness to share ideas is boundless. The famously busy Revd Dr Ayla Lepine nevertheless found time to comment on some of my chapters and share her wide-ranging knowledge of Gothic Revival art. And most especially, I would like to thank my friend and colleague, Dr Jennifer Johnson of St John's College, Oxford, who read a complete first draft and provided moral support.

Lastly, I would like to thank the modern stewards of Pugin's buildings – the house owners, institutions, and church congregations who care for this heritage.

David Frazer Lewis
Notre Dame, Indiana
January 2020

The river façade of the Houses of Parliament, designed by Charles Barry and A W N Pugin.
[© Historic England Archive AA077073]

Introduction

Augustus Welby Northmore Pugin's explosive rhetoric, ceaseless energy,
eccentric personal appearance, and zeal for the betterment of society all
capture the imagination.

His buildings hold an important place in national life: he decorated the
Houses of Parliament and steered the unwieldy ship of the Gothic Revival in
its transformation of the Victorian city.

Pugin was also much more than a designer of buildings. He was a
designer of beautiful objects in a vast array of media – metalwork, stained
glass, furniture, ceramic and stone. He was a theorist, a writer of powerful
rhetoric that gave order – and ardour – to the modernising of medieval
design. He was a religious reformer, sailor, set designer, antiquities
collector, businessman, and he was all of these things at once. It is even
safe to say that architecture was not Pugin's primary pursuit. From the
time of his conversion to Roman Catholicism in 1835, his main aim in life
was to contribute to the revival of Catholicism in Britain. As his biographer
Michael Trappes-Lomax wrote, 'it was God's glory he sought, not his own'.[1]
As an artist, he sought to further that revival through the arts, particularly
architecture.

Through Pugin's designs, church architecture was reborn, and house
design was transformed. He designed the first monastic buildings to be
built in Britain since the Reformation, and he suggested new forms for
urban life.

Pugin's church architecture sought to cast aside the cool intellectualism
of preaching-box Protestantism and re-establish a sensory experience of
religion. He wanted fragrant flowers, booming bells, and curling smoke. He
was the father of a tradition of Gothic Revivalists as liturgists, presenting
an all-encompassing vision for the Church. That said, Pugin did not single-
handedly launch the Gothic Revival, as is sometimes implied. There were
always others working in the style who shared his ideas, but he was a definite
leader. He made the Gothic Revival a movement.

It was Pugin's house designs that were the model for the suburban
Victorian villa – irregular brick buildings with gabled roofs and small

The only known photograph of A Welby Pugin. [Private Collection]

Frontispiece from *An Apology for the Revival of Christian Architecture*, showing idealised versions of Pugin's churches. [Public Domain]

gardens – which became an archetype of British housing. He helped popularise Gothic architecture for monastic and educational institutions, arguing that environments shaped character and could encourage certain behaviours. And finally, as one of the designers of the Houses of Parliament and author of several influential books on design, he helped to shape what the Victorian city would become as British industry and trade thrived in the second half of the 19th century.

Pugin saw himself as God's instrument, helping to repair a society damaged by industry and merchant greed. In contrast to the slums and poverty of the cities of his own day, which had little social safety net, Pugin believed that the Middle Ages provided a utopian model in which human

Pugin's childhood home in Bloomsbury,
106 Great Russell Street. [© Mr David March,
Historic England Archive IOE01_12856_11]

The drawing office of Pugin's father, Charles
Auguste Pugin. [Sworders]

dignity was respected and the destitute were cared for by the institutions of the Church. John Betjeman wrote that Pugin crafted a 'dream-like Middle Ages' as a response to his social conscience. Pugin later admitted that it was a Middle Ages of the imagination, with little grounding in historical reality.[2] But all utopias are founded on dreams.

Pugin was the only child of a French emigrant artist, Auguste Charles Pugin, and an English mother, Catherine Welby.[3] His friends and family called him Augustus, but as an adult he published under the name A Welby Pugin, emphasising the name of his English family alongside the purportedly Swiss aristocratic surname of his father's family. His father ran a drawing school in Bloomsbury, and Pugin assisted him from a young age.

By the time he was a teenager, he had demonstrated a precocious talent as a draughtsman. He had also shown a burgeoning interest in Gothic design, which he had learned by helping his father make measured drawings of Britain's medieval monuments as part of a project to publish a resource for architects and antiquarians seeking to develop their knowledge of Gothic art.[4]

In 1827, when Pugin was roughly the age of 14, a member of the firm of royal goldsmiths, Rundell and Bridge, discovered him drawing copies of Albrecht Dürer prints in the British Library.[5] As a result of the encounter, he was invited to design a Gothic chalice and then some Gothic furniture for George IV at Windsor. In 1829, Pugin began work as a stage carpenter for operas at Covent Garden and soon launched a career as a set designer. At the same time, he also founded a workshop that designed and produced furniture.

Although his furniture business failed in 1831, he married his first wife, Sarah Anne Garnett, that year.

Pugin's first daughter, Anne, was born in May of the following year, but her mother died a week later. Tragically, Pugin's father died at the end of the year, and his mother and beloved aunt, whom Pugin had often visited at the seaside in Ramsgate both died in 1833. Pugin found himself a widower and single father with a failed furniture business. Money left by his aunt and parents helped to support him through the grieving process. In mid-1833 he remarried, to a woman named Louisa Button, whom he seems to have met through the theatre. He then refocused his career, by determining to become an architect.

Pugin's architectural practice was rooted in drawing. The fluency and speed that he developed while assisting in his father's drawing school astonished contemporaries. His father often worked as an architectural perspectivist, translating architects' technical drawings into a picture of how a completed building would appear in its setting. Pugin's training was essentially as an artist of antiquarian bent.

An early Pugin furniture design. [Yale Center for British Art, Paul Mellon Collection B1977.14.20613]

He was never apprenticed to an architect. Yet drawing itself is a good way of understanding an object. In order to draw, one must see the way an object is put together, and that applies to buildings as well. He would send reams of rapid drawings and sketches to trusted craftsmen and builders, expecting them to work out the technicalities of making his vision a reality.

Pugin's architecture was also grounded in writing. He had a deep conviction that design was a philosophical process, and his explorations of architectural ideas would lead him to create a theoretical framework for Gothic architecture akin to that of the Classical orders. He drew out and explained its underlying logic, a logic that had been largely lost since the Middle Ages. In doing so, he also drew attention to what he believed were essential truths underlying all architecture, such as the importance of clear structural logic and the idea that one of architecture's functions is to

Measured drawing by the young A Welby Pugin of the conduit at the Bishop's Palace at Wells. [Yale Center for British Art, Paul Mellon Fund B1977.8.9]

affect the emotions. In today's architectural history, Pugin is regarded as a serious theoretician and intellect. Harvard's Neil Levine compares him to 19th-century French theorist Henri Labrouste.[6] He could write in English, French, and Latin, but his spelling was terrible in all three. This book has retained the quirky spelling used in his letters for the sake of authenticity.

Pugin's ideas evolved rapidly over his short career, and he would express embarrassment about his earliest works, many of which did not adhere to the rules of design he later constructed. Unlike some other writers on design, including John Ruskin (who became something of a rival), Pugin was able to write from a position of experience as both a designer and builder. Pugin's pronouncements about architecture in his 1843 book *The True Principles of Pointed or Christian Architecture* (hereafter *True Principles*) have become some of the most famous statements of Victorian design.[7]

In *True Principles*, Pugin laid down two laws of architecture: 'ist, that there should be no features about a building which are not necessary for convenience, construction, or propriety; 2nd, that all ornament should consist of the enrichment of the essential construction of the building'.[8] These were rules not merely for the design of Gothic buildings, but, he felt, universal architectural truths. For Pugin, Gothic architecture was best because it adhered to such universal architectural principles: honest construction; plan and elevation that reflected a building's use rather than an arbitrary symmetry; legible symbolism in its ornament; and most of all, moral purpose. He conceived architecture as a continuously developing tradition, and his job as an architect was simply to pick up where the Middle Ages left off.

Above all, Pugin believed that a building should be durably built. Watching the old Houses of Parliament burn as a young man had reinforced his belief in sound construction.

The ancient stone walls had withstood the blaze, but the modern brick and plaster walls cracked and split, showering sparks as they crashed to

Watercolour showing the smouldering remains of the Houses of Parliament after the 1834 fire by John Taylor Jr (1819–1884). [Yale Center for British Art, Paul Mellon Collection B1986.29.575]

7

the ground.[9] Gothic was both structural and pragmatic – expressing its construction and casting off water in a way appropriate to the climate of Northern Europe.

Ornament for Pugin was a given. Decoration was an integral ingredient of architecture because it was essential to its narrative purpose. It told the building's story. Ornament, Pugin explained, 'must possess an appropriate meaning' and must only be 'embellishment of that which is useful'.[10] It must not hide the reality of a building's structure but be an enrichment of the structure itself.

Stucco fronts, cast plaster decoration, and faux finishes were widespread in Regency England. Pugin's architecture, however, was built in durable, solid materials. He wrote that masonry construction called for arches – the lightest and most advanced load-bearing structure attainable with stone or brick. The flat lintels used by many classicists were not logical. For Pugin, this authenticity of material reflected the authenticity of Christian religion. The emotional effect created by his buildings, therefore, was rooted in transcendent reality.

Pugin's architecture was a total work of art. He saw decoration as integral to architecture, and he demanded stylistic consistency across all media. Stylistic consistency, after all, signalled consistency of ideas. He believed that Gothic was simpler and more authentic than other styles of architecture because it featured no superfluous constructed ornament, and it acknowledged human scale. He felt that furniture, just like buildings, should express its structure.

The expression of structure in built works would become accepted wisdom for many later architects. Louis Kahn, a mid-20th-century American architect famous for his command of pure form and natural light, subscribed to the tenet that, '[If] you say to brick, "what do you want, brick?" Brick says to you, "I like an arch."'[11] Kahn is unlikely to have traced the lineage of his ideas about honest construction through Pugin, although he undoubtedly deserves some of the credit for popularising such ideas. Only 50 years ago Pugin was a marginalised and somewhat unfashionable figure. That we know him much better today is thanks to the many people who have devoted themselves to the cause of Pugin (and he never allowed anyone to forget that he was a cause as well as an architect). His re-emergence is not the work of a few prominent taste-makers (though some of them have contributed), but rather the result of the many people who have been inspired by his designs or writings, the congregants who have lovingly cared for his churches, or the numerous scholars whose interest has been sparked. In a sense, his is a popular cause.

My task in writing this book is not to create any new insight *sui generis*, but rather to bring together the work of Pugin scholars of the last five decades to tell afresh the story of his architecture. Despite the publication of an excellent biography, the transcription, annotation, and publication of hundreds of his letters, the presentation of the data of his architectural output in a gazetteer, and numerous essays that have explored his roles in furniture design, liturgy, house design, and international architectural education, there has been no presentation of Pugin's architectural work in a short narrative format since Phoebe Stanton's *Pugin* of 1971.[12] In undertaking this work, I am standing on the shoulders of giants. I have gathered together what others have done in the hope that an updated narrative of Pugin's architectural career will help to introduce a new generation of readers to the works of this surprising and influential architect.

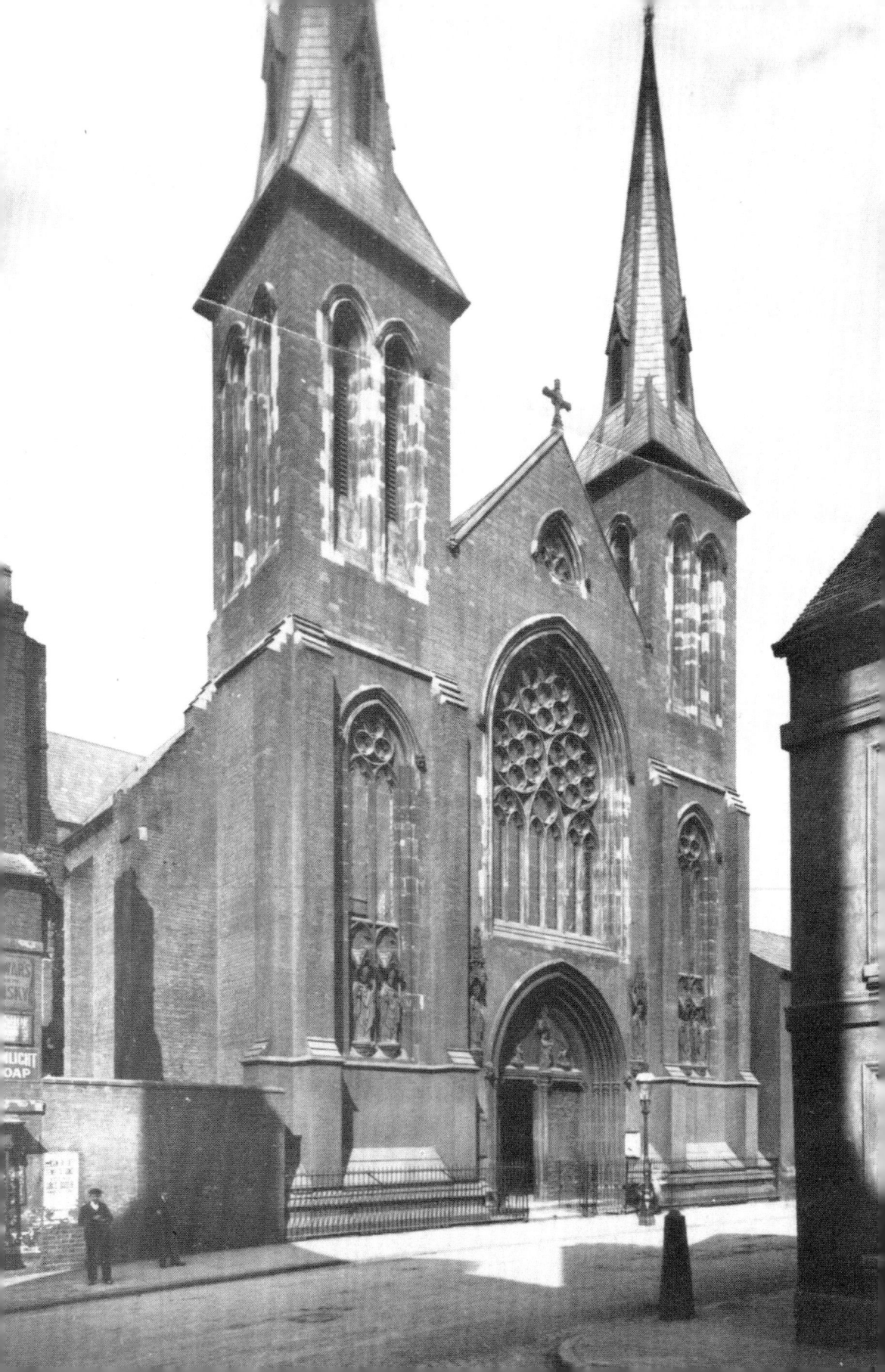

1 The house of God

Singing priests carrying boughs of hyssop and ampules of holy oil processed around the tall brick church. Above the huddled tiles and chimneys, a cross atop a single completed spire marked the spot of the procession below, and the crowds gathered in the streets to watch. The chanting ceased, and the pounding of the bishop's staff resounded thrice on the great oak doors. The iron hinges swung open and the bishop passed under reliefs of censing angels into his new church.

This could have been a medieval scene. But, although some of the clergy wore vestments of damask and gold thread cut in the Gothic style, much of the crowd wore top hats or hoop skirts and the words spoken included those of the modern Roman Catholic liturgy. This was Birmingham on 21 June 1841. The Roman Catholic clergy were gathered to consecrate St Chad's, the first church built in England since the Reformation that was intended to serve as a Roman Catholic cathedral. The return to the Middle Ages was deliberate, intended to signal that Catholic life was picking up again exactly where it had left off more than 300 years before.

Augustus Pugin, the architect of St Chad's, was only 26 years old when he designed it, yet he was already the author of half a dozen Catholic churches and Britain's leading Catholic church architect. The building was as big a statement as he could make with the limited budget.

Surrounded by the warehouses and tenements of the gun-making district, its crypt alone rose 40 feet above the Birmingham canal before it even reached the floor level of the chancel, whose roof stood another 80 feet above that. Its spire gave vitality to this otherwise somewhat depressed part of the city. Near its west façade, the high walls of the bishop's new palace implied a sort of piazza, creating a small Catholic world in front of the cathedral that seemed to draw the neighbourhood in around itself.

The church was built of brick because the congregation could not afford to build entirely of stone. Betjeman described it as 'soaring, impressive, and thin'.[1] It is hard to imagine today the impact it made in the mid-19th century. For although St Chad's is a handsome church, it is not in reality very large, and the setting on which its exterior effect depended has been

St Chad's Cathedral as it appeared in 1902. [Public Domain]

completely destroyed. During the Second World War, the gun-making district was bombed, with the church itself narrowly escaping destruction when a bomb fell through the roof. The bomb fractured some radiator pipes, and the water from the burst pipes extinguished the resulting fire. A painted panel in the ceiling marks the spot with the words 'Deo Gratia'. In the 1960s, planners cut the Birmingham Inner Ring Road through the damaged neighbourhood, passing only a few yards from the west doors of the cathedral and demolishing the Bishop's Palace in the process. The cathedral now stands divided from the central city by asphalt and traffic, forlorn among austerely landscaped empty lots.

The most generic sort of developer-modernist brick-veneered blocks align themselves to the new roads with no acknowledgement of the cathedral's presence. They are just tall enough to overshadow it. Large highway signs in front give directions to motorists. Whereas St Chad's was meant to signal the rising Christian tide among brute Victorian commercialism, a second wave of brute commercialism has washed back against it, and the cathedral stands stranded among the flotsam.

The setting of St Chad's Cathedral today. [Author]

Interior of St Chad's Cathedral. [Author]

The church is a hall church, meaning that its aisles are the same height as the nave. Therefore, it has no clerestory and the volume is unified by a single sweep of roof. The central mass is framed by the higher walls of the transepts and chancel at the east end and by the two towers and broach spires at the west. (The second spire was completed according to Pugin's design by his son Edward in 1856.) The form, Pugin said, was inspired by the brick cathedrals of Germany, particularly the Frauenkirche in Munich.[2] The distinct silhouette may also have been influenced by St Mary's Abbey Church at Reculver in Kent, an area of the coast that Pugin knew well, for its towers are much closer to St Chad's in proportion than the much taller towers of the German churches.[3]

It is the interior, however, on which Pugin concentrated his resources.

The interior, he felt, was the most important part of a church, where congregational worship itself took place. Visitors entering St Chad's for the first time are surprised by its loftiness. Tall slender piers line the nave, which Pugin made even lighter by bunching together tall narrow pillars rather than treating them as a single column. Because the aisles and naves share one roof, the pillars reach nearly all the way to the ceiling, a stone forest rising from a patterned floor of earthen tiles to a ceiling canopy painted with foliage and stars. The ceiling feels taut like a tent canopy stretched over a matchstick framework. It could not be anything except Victorian. The product of modern engineering of lightweight processed timbers, it whispers of the balloon frame more than of the hammer beam. The crossing and transepts express themselves by rows of pillars only – the hall church format means that the interior reads as a single unified rectangular volume.

At the end of the nave, drawing the eye with its bright stained glass and pillars gilded with barber's pole stripes, is the chancel, the centrepiece of the church, where the high altar stands bearing the golden casket of the bones of St Chad.

The altar is crowned by a high carved and gabled canopy and flanked, in the manner of a medieval English altar, by damask curtains between tall riddel posts topped with kneeling angels bearing tapers. From the outset, Pugin intended that the chancel should be screened. This screen, Pugin felt, was essential to proper worship, and when his patron Bishop Walsh suggested that it might not be in keeping with modern Catholic practice, Pugin threatened to resign.[4] The chancel screen at St Chad's was donated by his great friend, the metalwork and stained-glass maker John Hardman. Pugin fixed 15th-century statues to it, and on top he placed a rood, of which only the giant crucifix survives today, suspended from the chancel arch. Architecturally, the screen meant that the whole space of the church was not revealed at once, creating a sense of mystery. It meant that even once a worshipper took a seat in the nave for the service, it still felt as

The High Altar of St Chad's Cathedral before later removal of some original fittings.
[© Historic England Archive AA42/00175]

if there was further to go; it gave a sense of journeying into the church as
the service progressed. Liturgically, the screen acted as a sort of window
from the metaphorical earth of the nave into the metaphorical heaven of
the sanctuary. Pugin would later write a treatise defending chancel screens.

They were a feature he felt most passionately about, and their gradual disappearance from post-Reformation Catholic ritual he believed was a corruption. Screens were a topic that would cause him great heartache, for the official Roman Catholic position never aligned with his own. Whereas he felt that screens enhanced the mystery of the Mass, most British bishops felt that they detracted from it by blocking the congregation's view.

Pugin's concept

St Chad's was a turning point for Pugin because it was here that all the features that would mark his mature design practice appeared together in a highly visible church. Pugin had designed his first complete church in 1837 at the age of 25 and St Chad's was completed and opened by the time he was 29. This is remarkable not only because of his young age, but because over the course of those four years he had essentially laid a path for the future of the Gothic Revival. St Chad's was a true wonder at a time when antiquarian understanding of the Middle Ages was still emerging. Technical knowledge of Gothic structure and a sense of the chronology of Gothic design were discoveries of the previous 50 years and were still being developed.[5] The first recorded use of the word medieval was in 1827.[6] Pugin's father, Auguste Charles Pugin, and his generation had laid the groundwork by measuring and recording surviving Gothic architecture, thus making the empirical reality of surviving medieval structures available for study. Auguste Pugin was best known for illustrating *The Microcosm of London* with Thomas Rowlandson, but he then dedicated his later career to publishing large volumes of measured drawings of Gothic buildings and artefacts.[7] Young Augustus Pugin spent his childhood in pursuit of this knowledge, scrambling over the roofs and walls of medieval buildings taking measurements with his father's pupils.

Besides its more authentic medieval aesthetic, what made Pugin feel that St Chad's was a relative success was that it contained all the fittings and spaces necessary for the Use of Sarum. The Use of Sarum was the distinctive form of worship practiced by English Catholics, the medieval liturgy of the Diocese of Salisbury, which had been used over most of southern England until it was finally banned after the reign of Mary I. (The Anglican *Book of Common Prayer* that replaced it was itself influenced by the patterns of English medieval worship.[8]) Pugin was overwhelmed by the beauty and mystery of this type of liturgy, which leaned more heavily on ceremonial than the services he had experienced as a child in the early 19th century. It called, for instance, for several vested deacons, censing of many altars, cross-bearers, suspended lights, and numerous acolytes bearing candles. The type of altar used at St Chad's was the type specified by the Sarum Use, an altar flanked by curtains and riddel posts and decorated with cross and candles. Although long banished from Protestant churches, the appearance of these medieval altars was preserved in prints and paintings, just as the Sarum Use itself was recorded in surviving late medieval books.

Pugin had first been attracted to the Catholic Church by the splendid ceremonial of the medieval Church at its height, and he was disappointed after his conversion to discover the modest spaces and simpler Tridentine (modern Roman) ceremonial of the newly legal English Catholic chapels. He devoted himself from that point onwards to restoring the glory of the medieval church, not only for aesthetic reasons, but because he believed that it represented a sort of religious technology.[9] What Pugin felt he had discovered was an aesthetic tradition whose every form and furnishing was designed to support and encourage Christian passion. He learned the details of this medieval system by reading the works of medieval liturgists such as Durandus, a 13th-century French bishop who recorded the symbolic meanings assigned to every part of the medieval church, and by talking to the Revd Dr Daniel Rock, a scholar of medieval liturgy and chaplain to Pugin's most significant patron, the Earl of Shrewsbury.

One of the paradoxes of Pugin is that he was at once both pragmatic and profoundly Romantic. There is no denying that Pugin was a product of the Romantic Movement, for one of the main goals of his designs was to provoke the aesthetic imagination through a felt change of consciousness – to take those encountering his buildings outside themselves so that they could have an encounter with the spiritual. 'Few persons ...', he wrote, 'can enter [a Gothic church] without experiencing some feelings of reverential awe'.[10] He believed that the medieval church had found a formula for inciting this sort of experience. The revival of medieval forms was therefore in that sense an entirely functional concern. Pugin knew the value of a tall spire with chiming bells as a landmark and a call to prayer, of the grand raised altar as theatre of the Eucharist, of the gloomy side chapel for private prayer. Pan-European Christendom over hundreds of years had developed a tradition of building that was best fit for purpose, a rich text of symbols that triggered emotions and reverence. Contemporary utilitarians would have scorned this idea, for Pugin's concerns were not pragmatic. However, he believed that the function of a church was largely to trigger an emotional response to the presence of God. He was seeking an architecture of affect.[11]

In seeking to revive Catholic devotion, Pugin hoped to inspire the sort of moral behaviours that were in keeping with Christian principles. His Gothic dream was one in which the shortcomings of Victorian commercial society – the cruelty of the poor laws and the darkness and pollution of the crowded industrial cities – would be cast away by the social cooperation and charity springing from religious revival. As early as 1843 he wrote to his friend J R Bloxam, 'This revival of Catholic architecture is producing a

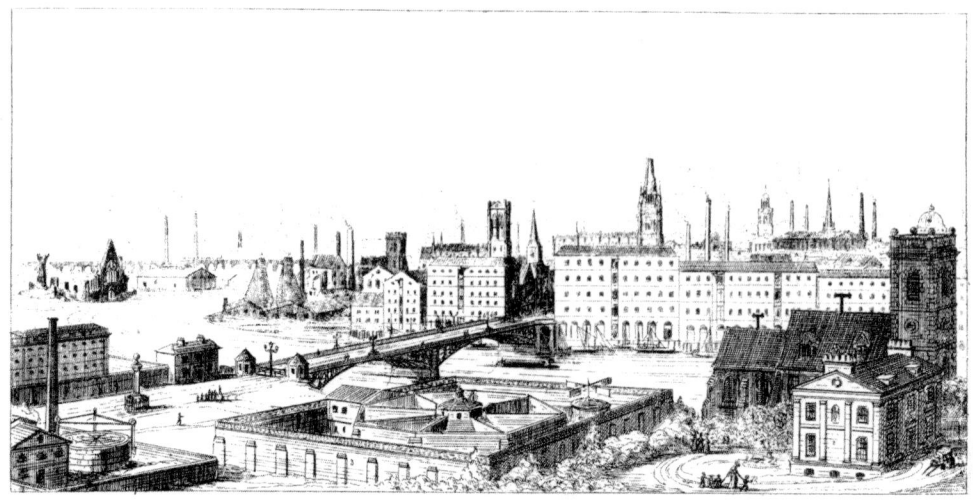

THE SAME TOWN IN 1840

1. St Michael's Tower, rebuilt in 1750. 2. New Parsonage House & Pleasure Grounds. 3. The New Jail. 4. Gas Works. 5. Lunatic Asylum. 6. Iron Works & Ruins of St Marie's Abbey. 7. Mr Evans Chapel. 8. Baptist Chapel. 9. Unitarian Chapel. 10. New Church. 11. New Town Hall & Concert Room. 12. Wesleyan Centenary Chapel. 13. New Christian Society. 14. Quakers Meeting. 15. Socialist Hall of Science.

Catholic town in 1440.

1. St Michaels on the Hill. 2. Queens Cross. 3. St Thomas's Chapel. 4. St Maries Abbey. 5. All Saints. 6. St Johns. 7. St Peters. 8. St Alkmunds. 9. St Maries. 10. St Edmunds. 11. Grey Friars. 12. St Cuthberts. 13. Guild hall. 14. Trinity. 15. St Olaves. 16. St Botolphs.

An illustration from Pugin's *Contrasts*, comparing an imaginary town of the Middle Ages to its state in the present day. [Public Domain]

great moral change'.[12] In the second edition of his book *Contrasts*, published that same year, he called for almshouses where the poor could be cared for, fed and given Christian burials, in contrast to the cells and forced labour of the workhouses. He called for beautiful cities defined by stone spires and pinnacles in pristine natural environments, in which the main social institutions were church-based rather than profit-driven.

Pugin believed that it was buildings that allowed for social change – new institutions had to have appropriate facilities. Architecture was thereby a moral force. This was Pugin's revolution.

The idea that architecture was a moral force was not unique, and had been suggested by philosophers since the early modern age.[13] But Pugin was the clarion call. His books laid out apparently practical examples of how architecture could lead to social reform. Of all his contemporaries, his Gothic dream was the most lucid, and it fired the enthusiasm of a whole generation fuelled by the desire for social reform, so that over the following decades, Britain's cities rose up in towers and pinnacles crowned with gilded vanes. The Gothic Revival was an architectural idea that bridged the political spectrum: country landowners could host great pageants for their tenants and imagine their fields ringing with song from a new church, and reformers could build hammer-beamed halls in which to train craftsmen and feed the hungry of Dickensian cities. It was an image on which Disraeli could hang his Toryism at Hughenden or Morris his Socialism at Kelmscott. Medievalism reached from the slums of Manchester to the Wood Beyond the World.

Yes, it looked backwards, but the critics who have faulted this have forgotten to walk round and see that, like Janus, it also had a face on the other side, looking with equal intensity towards the future. Later Gothic Revivalists would argue that all one has on which to build the future is the past.

Pugin's early churches

In his first churches, Pugin was developing a vocabulary that could carry his primary goal for the Revival – no less than the rebirth of medieval Catholic ritual in England. For the first years of his career as an architect, Pugin's idea was simply to bring back the Middle Ages. He had yet to develop the subtleties of architectural principle that would later explain how he felt this could best be achieved.

Pugin's career as an architect began with a bang; between 1837 and 1839 he was commissioned to design more than a dozen churches. Now that enough time had passed since the 1829 Catholic Emancipation Act for Catholic institutions to begin to be established, there was large demand for new Roman Catholic churches across England. Through his writings, Pugin had quickly secured a place as the foremost Catholic architect in

St James's, Reading, before later alterations. [Historic England Archive HT01859]

the country. His book *Contrasts*, the first edition of which was published in 1836, was exceedingly popular, and in 1837 he was appointed Professor of Ecclesiastical Antiquities at the seminary of Oscott – the beating heart of the Catholic missionary effort. His first church was St James's, Reading, a small neo-Norman affair begun in 1837.

His first Gothic church was the Church of the Assumption at Bree, County Wexford, begun in 1838, which featured the first open wooden roof to be built in Ireland in modern times.[14] Pugin's initial concept of Gothic was quite wide-ranging; he was happy to draw from any pre-Reformation source in Britain or abroad. Among his early churches, some chancels were apsidal (a feature that was rare in medieval England, but common on the Continent) and some were square-ended. He drew from Norman, Early English, German of all periods, and the late Perpendicular Gothic of Oxford and Winchester. In the case of Reading, he chose Norman to complement the Norman ruins of Reading Abbey, over whose foundations, to Pugin's horror, part of the new church complex was actually built.[15] The neo-Tudor Reading Gaol would later be built by the firm of George Gilbert Scott directly behind Pugin's church. Response to context was one of Pugin's design principles from the start.[16]

Both St James's and the Church of the Assumption were simple and small, and Pugin felt he made significant progress in the design of his church at St Mary's, Uttoxeter, the first of his churches to open and the first to be funded by his major patron, Lord Shrewsbury. Pugin described it as 'the first Catholic structure erected in this country in strict accordance with the rules of ancient ecclesiastical architecture, since the days of the pretended reformation'.[17] It, and its successor, St Mary's, Derby, reveal that his initial priority was to build churches equipped for ritualistic worship, for here we find the raised chancels, splendid high altars, soaring proportions, and shared benches in long naves.

The only element of his mature principles missing from these churches was a chancel screen. St Alban's, Macclesfield, a large parish church opened in 1841, was the first designed with a screen and from then on he almost always used them.[18] Screens, he had learned, were essential to the Sarum Use.[19]

St Mary's, Derby. [© Historic England Archive AA42/00876]

Interior of St Mary's, Derby. The iron chancel screen is in keeping with Pugin's preferences. [© Historic England Archive AA42/00883]

In his early churches, his detailing was better than that of his less archaeologically inclined colleagues, but his buttresses were somewhat thin, his
churches boxy and often awkwardly placed behind towers that were too wide
for them. His plans tended toward symmetry, with a tower at the centre of
the west front, and if he had sufficient funds, two aisles flanking a wider
nave. Such a plan was not much different from the arrangements he had
condemned in the work of his Gothick colleagues. The chancel, at least, he
usually defined as a separate exterior volume, its roof a step lower than the
roof of the nave. His concern at the time was not with innovative plan, but
first with chancels properly furnished with the equipment for the liturgy,
and second, with soaring proportions, which he felt were essential to Gothic
architecture, both as a symbol of the Resurrection and as a way of triggering
the emotions of worshippers. The attribution of emotional effect to the
soaring proportions of the Gothic church appeared in his earliest published
writings. He explained that the exterior of a Gothic church should be

> well calculated to awaken those sentiments of reverence and devotion,
> suited to the holy place. But if the exterior of the temple be so soul-
> stirring, what a burst of glory meets the eye, on entering a long majestic
> line of pillars rising into lofty and fretted vaulting ... cold, indeed, must
> be the heart of man who does not cry out with the Psalmist, Domine
> dilexi decorem domus tuae, et locum habitationis gloriae tuae.[20]

Pugin's True Principles

Pugin was a restless character 'always flyin' about like a locomotive', and
his architecture was an architecture for activity: chanting, censing, praying,
smelling, seeing.[21] The rebirth of Catholic England, Pugin felt, required
urgent and decisive action. In contrast to the polite perambulations of
genteel sightseers in 18th-century prints, Pugin portrayed his churches
teeming with procession and worship.

The cool, contemplative Gothic of the later revivalists such as G F Bodley,
who built places to listen in silence for a still, quiet voice, was not Pugin's
own. His churches have an embodied energy. Much of the action was
sensory – the celebration of Creation by experiencing it. The Lady Chapel at
Ushaw had bright brass vases for lilies bolted along the screen and hooks
in the walls for hanging floral garlands on major feast days.[22] The fittings
themselves demanded interaction: gathering and placing flowers, lighting
candles so that their light danced over the stones and tiles, ringing a bronze
bell to announce the transformation of wine into Christ's blood.

Because of this concern with a given set of activities, namely the sensory
ritual of the Sarum Use, there were certain features which Pugin's mature

An illustration from Pugin's *Glossary of Ecclesiastical Ornament*, showing an ideal church in use.
[Public Domain]

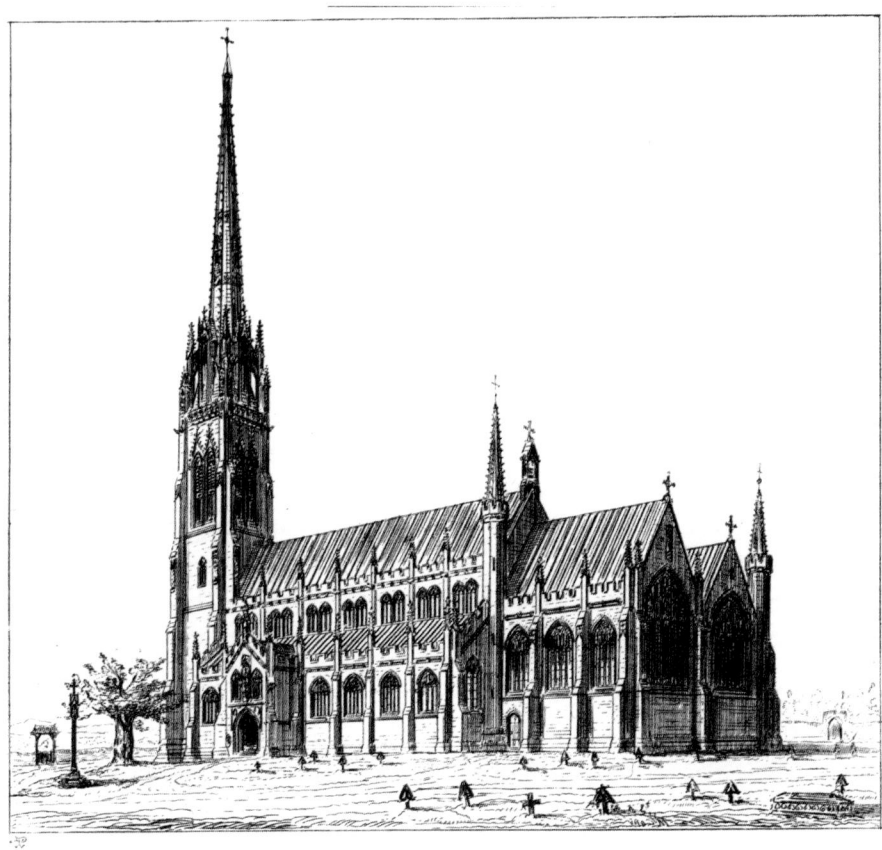

Pugin's ideal church, as illustrated in *True Principles*. [Public Domain]

churches always included. His ideal church could be described as follows. A tall spire marked the location of the church, which symbolically pointed to heaven and symbolised the Resurrection.

Out of 30 churches Pugin designed with towers, only 7 were not intended to have spires.[23] Whether or not a church had a tower was usually determined by size – he generally gave small churches a bellcote instead. The church was entered via a porch near the west end. Since medieval weddings and baptisms began in the porch, the architect treated it as sacred space and adorned it with relevant imagery. Passing through the porch into the church, a baptistry would be located nearby, symbolising the beginning of the spiritual journey. Rather than simply having a font sitting at the back of an aisle, Pugin preferred for the baptistry to be a defined space, screened off, with the font raised on a dais. An aisle or aisles, if present, led to screened chapels at the east end. Chancels were deep enough to hold choir stalls and, in the English fashion, terminated in a flat rather than curving wall. The

Sedilia, St Giles', Cheadle. [Author]

most elaborate decoration was in the chancel because that was where the most important ceremonies took place. In his early churches, chancels would contain all the features mentioned in the Sarum Missal, including sedilia, stone niches that provided seats for officiating clergy near the altar.

He also liked to include an Easter sepulchre, a decorated niche in which the entombment of Jesus could be re-enacted during Holy Week. Both these features were expensive, and in the case of the Easter sepulchre, rarely used, so Pugin moved away from them in his later designs. In large churches, transepts would be included, making their plans cruciform.[24]

This ideal church was a formula that Pugin had developed. It was the engine of his religious technology, a structural-symbolic system that he had carefully extracted from medieval sources and refined for Victorian practice. He shared that system in a trilogy of important books. *Contrasts*, his original 1836 bestseller, identified the problem; it explained why the Gothic Revival was needed and presented alluring images of what he hoped it could achieve. He updated it and reissued it in 1841. *True Principles* explained the system for reviving Gothic architecture – how Gothic was structured, what it was made of, what spaces it needed to contain, and how to design its details.[25] It was published in 1841. Then in 1844, *A Glossary of Ecclesiastical Ornament*, a dictionary of Catholic art, laid out the history and functions of a vast array of liturgical objects and vestments.[26] It also illustrated the traditional forms of images used as symbolic ornament in churches and explained their meaning.

Pugin wanted to spread his revival, and here were his lessons. 'Building, without teaching and explaining', he wrote, 'is useless'.[27] He already had several years of experience lecturing on this material at Oscott, and as a consequence the books were masterpieces of exposition. They were partly a typical Victorian project in the organisation of knowledge: Pugin, archaeologist and antiquary, collecting and organising the material of a lost civilisation by close study of physical remains and textual evidence. But the project went much further than mere typology. Most surprisingly for those used to thinking of Gothic as rude and barbarous, it presented a rational system that rivalled the Classical tradition of Vitruvius and Palladio, a tradition developed over hundreds of years to be fit for purpose, broken down into precepts that he claimed gave insight into the nature of architecture itself.

St Giles', Cheadle

Pugin demonstrated his system with his finest church to date: St Giles', Cheadle in north Staffordshire.

Begun in 1841 and completed in 1846, he called it 'Perfect Cheadle, my consolation in all afflictions'.[28] He wrote, 'It will raise the dignity of religion amazingly'.[29]

Interior of St Giles', Cheadle. [Author]

The imaginary ideal Pugin church described above might as well have been a description of Cheadle. Its nave was flanked by two aisles. At the end of the north aisle was a Lady Chapel, at the end of the south aisle was a Chapel of the Blessed Sacrament. The screened chancel featured sedilia and an Easter sepulchre. There was no clerestory, but the aisles were roofed separately from the nave. The spire at the west end was aligned with the east–west liturgical axis of the church.

Although the concept was, in a sense, nothing new, the presentation of it was his best to date. The spire soared 200 feet over a town where the buildings were seldom higher than 40 feet. The massive stone walls were carved in fine detail – crockets of curling leaves, lions along the string courses, corbels of kings' heads, pinnacles, niches, and tracery. It was set down in a medieval world of its own; no Georgian houses or iron lampposts jostled against its walls. A stone cross topped with the figures of the Virgin Mary, St John the Evangelist, and Christ crucified marked the sacred ground of the churchyard. Beyond the boundary walls were the lead-covered wooden belfries of a Pugin-designed school and convent. Inside, the church was alive with colour and ornament. The detail and decoration were exquisite and executed in fine materials. Even within the same pier, wall, or floor, the rich patterning changed constantly – stars to rays to lions to crosses

Detail of stencilling, St Giles', Cheadle. [Author]

to crowns – every area of the church had a unique colour scheme, usually picked out in gilding.

The result was a warm glow all around. The effect was so stunning that when John Henry Newman entered the church for the first time he exclaimed, 'Porta coeli!'[30]

Pugin had grown into his own principles and finally had the budget to express them fully. The thinness of his previous churches was gone. Instead of matchsticks, the ceiling timbers were like the underside of one of his table designs, full of X-braces and curves. To quote *True Principles*, 'the principal tie-beams, rafters, purloins, and braces, which in modern edifices are hidden at vast expense by a flat plaster ceiling, are here rendered very ornamental features'.[31] The external buttresses were massive, 'so as to produce a fine effect of light and shade', with each one diminishing 'naturally as it rises and has less to resist'.[32] And whereas he had had to leave previous churches only partially furnished and decorated for lack of funds, Cheadle was completely furnished to his designs by craftsmen with whom he would work for the rest of his career.

The success of Cheadle was not simply a matter of the features present, but of how they were crafted. The metalwork was by John Hardman of Birmingham. Hardman worked closely with Pugin to develop methods of

West doors of St Giles', Cheadle, flanked by carvings by Thomas Roddis. [Author]

metalworking and, eventually, from 1845, stained glass-making that used modern methods to approximate medieval techniques.[33] The floors were by Herbert Minton of Stoke-on-Trent, who had revived the craft of encaustic tile making, in which different coloured clays are fired together to make the pattern. This creates a tile in which the decorative pattern is not merely painted on but integral to the tile itself and therefore does not wear off. The sculpture was carved by Thomas Roddis, Pugin's favourite mason, who, to Pugin's great distress, died in 1845 before Cheadle was completed. (Pugin designed a small monument to him in the north porch.) And George Myers, Pugin's trusted Southwark-based builder, translated Pugin's few sketches into high-quality masonry and timber work. That Pugin's churches have a distinctive atmosphere is the product not solely of his principles, which were shared and imitated by other architects, but of this particular team of craftsmen, who executed his designs faithfully for many years.

Material and locality

Every design had to be appropriate to its material, and Pugin was a master of many.[34] He designed braced oak tables and gates with curves that remembered the shape of the branches; bright brass grates whose solid bars of different thickness spiralled into ornament; and sculptural stone mouldings appropriate to their structural position and water-repelling function. By the standards of the time, his brickwork too was craftsmanly, run in careful English bond that broke into patterns to enliven blank expanses of wall. This 'honesty' to material would be echoed by John Ruskin, William Morris, and the proponents of the Arts and Crafts Movement.

In a surprising pre-emption of the Arts and Crafts Movement, Pugin even began to feel his way into a belief that materials should be locally sourced and used in a way that reflected local building traditions. He knew intuitively that the use of local materials would make a building a better complement to its neighbours and prevent monotony as building materials began to be distributed nationally via the railways. Cheadle nestles comfortably in its valley, contrasting sharply with many of the churches of his contemporaries whose frontispiece west ends were placed parallel to the street. His church of St Augustine, Ramsgate, which is built of knapped flint in the tradition of Kent, and the rough granite of his County Wexford churches harmonise beautifully with their settings.

'[The] ancient builders', Pugin explained, '[adapted] their edifices to localities, [so] that they seemed as if they formed a portion of nature itself … growing from the sites in which they were placed'.[35]

Cheadle was also local in that it looked exclusively to English precedent, from its square-ended chancel to its Decorated tracery and sedilia. The

Detail of the knapped flint and ashlar façade of St Augustine's, Ramsgate. [Author]

commitment to specifically English forms for specifically English liturgies was largely the result of the influence of the Revd Dr Rock. Pugin was amenable to that influence because it fitted with his own interests and studies. Over the course of his career, his promotion of English medieval forms rather than modern Roman ones would cause friction with a number of Catholic leaders both in England and in the Papal States. Pugin wrote in 1842, when Cheadle had been under construction for about a year, 'our ancestors were not Roman Catholic, they were English catholics. Of course in communion with Rome. We have had an English Church from the days of Blessed Austin'.[36]

Pugin was suspicious of the universalising aspect of Classicism, which he felt had become entrenched in architecture across Europe. His vision of a worldwide Christendom was one in which local artistic and liturgical practice reflected varying histories and national characteristics. He decried

the extraordinary amalgamation of architecture, style, and manners now in progress, that were it not for the works of nature which cannot be destroyed, and the glorious works of Christian antiquity which have *not* yet been destroyed, Europe would soon present such sameness as to cease to be interesting. Already a sort of bastard Greek, a nondescript modern style, has ravaged many of the most interesting cities of Europe; replacing the original national buildings with unmeaning lines of plaster fronts.[37]

Ireland

Working according to this principle and within his limited knowledge of medieval Irish architecture, Pugin tried to incorporate the artistic tradition of the medieval Irish Church into his designs in Ireland. The result is a group of churches that are in some ways unlike Pugin's other work.

They introduced the fully-fledged Gothic Revival to a country where church-building practice was thoroughly Georgianised, the standard rural church consisting of a single-cell 'preaching barn' with a plaster ceiling and plaster decorations.[38]

Pugin was particularly excited by Ireland, admiring the people's devoted Catholic faith. He travelled there nearly every year, but generally only for brief stays, meaning that his works were left in the hands of local builders who, without easy access to the architect, sometimes strayed from his intentions. Nevertheless, his influence was tremendous – not only through his involvement at St Peter's College, County Wexford, and St Patrick's Seminary, Maynooth, County Kildare, but also via his articles in *The Dublin Review* and the *Catholic Directory*, which was sent to every Catholic priest in the country.[39]

The interior of St Mary's Cathedral, Killarney. [Richard Butler]

The Hardman metalworks firm in Birmingham reported getting large numbers of orders for Pugin-designed church plate from Ireland throughout the 1840s. Clearly his brand was well known.

Unlike England, Ireland had a recognised Catholic hierarchy, and his two grandest commissions there were for cathedrals at Enniscorthy and Killarney. St Aidan's, Enniscorthy, County Wexford, was begun in 1843, and because of its limited budget, took an abbey church rather than a medieval cathedral as its ultimate model.

The plan was based on Tintern Abbey, whose Irish daughter house was located nearby.[40] The Irish Tintern was probably also the source for the

St Aidan's Cathedral, Enniscorthy. [Richard Butler]

A distant view of St Mary's, Killarney. [Richard Butler]

crow-stepped battlements and square crossing tower at St Michael's, Gorey,
County Wexford. Sited on a hill rising from within the boundaries of the
town, Pugin gave St Aidan's a broach spire to mark its place on the skyline.

By contrast, Pugin's other Irish cathedral, St Mary's, Killarney, County
Kerry, was located on a plain that must have reminded him of Salisbury; he
therefore designed a towering spire (although this was not completed until
1912).

With roughly the same ground area as St Aidan's, St Mary's tall walls give
it a stronger sense of verticality. Its detailing, as in all Pugin's Irish churches,
is simple, and its mouldings are inspired by those of nearby Muckross
Abbey.[41]

In plan and proportion, Pugin's Irish churches were similar to his other
work. The large parish church of St Michael's at Gorey, designed in 1839, was
cruciform in plan with the square tower at the crossing intended to carry
a spire. St Alphonsus', Barntown, County Wexford, was a mid-size double-
aisled church with a bellcote. But the decoration was much more sparing,
even austere. There were round arches; tracery was rare. Round stair towers
were a nod to Irish monastic architecture. Pugin wrote that Irish medieval
architecture was often 'rude and simple; but, massive and solemn they

Detail of St Mary's, Tagoat, showing Pugin's Irish stonework. [David O'Leary]

St Mary's, Tagoat. [David O'Leary]

harmonised most perfectly with [their] wild and rocky localities'.[42] His study of the ruins of Dunbrody Abbey, County Wexford, particularly, which was near the home of his Wexford patrons, was reflected in the rough granite walling and limestone trim of his Irish churches.

Pugin admired the work of Irish masons, and it was in his Irish churches that he first began to experiment with the massive walls that would come to define his later work.[43]

The greatest surprise was his deliberate cultivation of the archaic. The pier capitals in the nave at Tagoat, County Wexford, were carved with stiff, almost diagrammatic leaves that evoke the rough cushion capitals surviving at Glendalough and Cashel. Pugin was seeking atmosphere in addition to liturgical function. Archaism is the last thing one would expect of Pugin, who happily broke with the precedents of medieval art in order to have anatomically correct sculpted and painted figures in his English churches (an instantly distinguishable mark of the Victorian Gothic Revival). Local character, it seems, trumped all.

Australia

However, in 1845, around the same time as Pugin was at work on the cathedrals of Killarney and Enniscorthy, he began work on a series of churches that at first glance seemed to break this rule entirely. These were the group of small churches that would be built to Pugin's designs by Roman Catholics in Australia. Nothing seems more incongruous than coming across a small Puginian church on a Tasmanian rise!

Although the vista may at first look English, with the bellcote rising among the sheep, this particular church is located halfway around the world in the part of Australia nearest to Antarctica.

Why then, in the most exotic setting imaginable, did Pugin make his churches perfectly English? The answer must be that in designing churches for a place with no existing Christian tradition, churches that were to be built by Englishmen, he decided that the English tradition was the one to carry with them. It would be left to later Gothic Revivalists with more information about the new country and experience of missionary work among the Indigenous people (and New Zealand Maori) to develop Gothic churches in Oceania that responded to local traditions.[44]

That is not to say that these Australian churches were the perfect twins of Pugin's English ones. They were rougher, smaller, and the product of a newly settled frontier rather than the work of skilled craftsmen with access to established networks of manufacturing in nearby industrial cities. And yet they contained all the essential features of Pugin's religious technology – the raised, decorated chancel, lofty proportions, exposed timber ceilings, porches, and baptismal fonts near the west end. The newly

St Paul's, Oatlands, Tasmania. [Archdiocese of Hobart Archives and Heritage Collection]

designated Bishop of Hobart Town, Robert Wilson, had worked quickly and closely with Pugin, for he had to sail on a certain date, to plan a way that the Catholic Revival could be carried to Australia. Recognising the limitations that local builders would face in the young settlements, Pugin designed a set of ideal churches and sent the drawings with Bishop Wilson. He also had three wooden models of churches made that fit together to show how the churches should be constructed. The hope was that local builders could use the models to replicate the true principle of 'honest' construction. Wilson's supervisor, John Polding, the Bishop of Sydney, also ordered plans and fittings for similarly-scaled small churches from Pugin via an English agent.

In Australia, with no existing 'corruptions' (ie non-medieval building or fittings) such as those Pugin complained loudly about in England and Ireland, a Catholic society could be built around the medieval model in the first instance. Here, Pugin dared to hope, his utopian view of a Christian society could be realised by a bishop who 'had departed across the ocean to the antipodes, carrying the seeds of Christian design to grow and flourish in the New World'.[45] With characteristic zeal, Pugin set out to spread his Gothic Revival around the world.

Gothic triumphant

With his books, and with Cheadle, Pugin hoped to inspire his fellow archi-tects to take on the mantle of the Gothic Revival. And he was successful. Interest in Cheadle was substantial. Other architects made special trips to visit the building site, including George Gilbert Scott. Descriptions of the new church were published across Europe. The European world was looking to see what this major Protestant nation's resurgence of Roman Catholicism would look like, and the church's opening was attended by the editors of French and German journals of ecclesiastical design.[46] Sir Charles Barry, lead architect of the new Houses of Parliament, was there too.

Pugin did not single-handedly generate the Gothic Revival. He is sometimes thought of (and this is largely a result of his own self-presen-tation) as a voice crying in the wilderness, but his message would not have been so popular if others had not already been thinking along the same lines – both in Britain and abroad. For Pugin was responding to something that was already beginning to happen in France, the Low Countries, and Germany, as well as among British antiquarians. The combination of factors that included the Romantic Movement, the problems of industriali-sation, rising nationalism, and the desire for liturgical change among many branches of Christianity, were factors affecting all of Europe, and much of the rest of the world as well, during the turbulent decade of the 1840s. His pupil John Hardman Powell wrote: 'He came at just the right time. Sir Walter Scott had Medievalized poetic-story; Christian Archaeologists and Antiquarians were forming associations, articles and controversies in Periodicals kept the subject alive; and so his work rose on the crest of a wave of public interest'.[47]

Pugin never claimed to be original. John Henry Newman's influential church at Littlemore in Oxfordshire is just one example of archaeologically correct Gothic Revival, equipped for ritual and laden with symbolism, built by other architects before Pugin designed his first church in 1837.[48]

It was even suggested, at a time when Pugin was still a living memory, that his earliest churches took inspiration from Littlemore's plan and form, for here were the single-gabled cell, open timber ceiling, and focus on the altar (but not the chancel screen) that would make up much of Pugin's own formula for small churches. Victorian vicars read their buildings as symbolic texts before Pugin presented himself as a new Durandus, nor was he the only architect to suggest that an essential function of a church was to trigger an emotional response in the worshipper.[49]

St Mary and St Nicholas, Littlemore, designed by H J Underwood. [Henry Taunt/Historic England Archive CC73/01181]

Yet somehow Pugin's was the voice that rang out over the din and clamour of his age – at least when it came to his fellow architects. When any British Gothicist from the height of Pugin's career onwards was asked to name his greatest inspiration, nearly every one of them said Pugin. Sir George Gilbert Scott, architect of the Albert Memorial and the Midland Grand Hotel at London's St Pancras Station, would proclaim that Pugin 'was our leader and our most able pioneer'.[50] Reading Pugin had converted Scott to the Gothic and transformed his career. He would be Pugin's closest successor in terms of his facility in the design of church furnishings and in the sheer volume of his output (which, unlike Pugin, he achieved by hiring an enormous number of assistants); his churches hovered more towards Puginian rectitude than those of most of his colleagues. He instructed that Pugin be prominently memorialised among the British architects carved on the base of the Albert Memorial (a structure, with its trumpeting of secular glory, that Pugin would have disliked), receiving Queen Victoria's permission to place Pugin at the corner – the literal cornerstone of the High Victorian architectural world.[51]

William Butterfield, who would go on to design the Argyle-jumper-patterned brickwork of Keble College, Oxford, began his career ordering stained glass and fittings for his first churches directly from Pugin. He would translate the painted patterns of Cheadle into a more durable structural polychromy through the use of coloured bricks and terra cotta. In Ireland, where Pugin's influence was, as we will see, largely propagated through the seminary he designed at Maynooth in County Kildare, J J McCarthy would take up his principles so faithfully that he would earn the nickname 'the

Sculpture of Pugin at the corner of the Albert Memorial. [Author]

The Basilica of the Holy Blood, Bruges, Belgium, as redecorated by Jean-Baptiste Bethune.
[Steven Slaubaugh]

Irish Pugin'.[52] Dozens, even hundreds, of less famous High Victorian architects would draw from Pugin's ideas, with smaller budgets and varying
grasps of medieval design, to raise pointed arches across the English-
speaking world, not just in Australia but Canada and antebellum Alabama.[53]

On the Continent, Pugin's closest disciple was Jean-Baptiste Bethune, who met and corresponded with him and kept a framed photograph of the master in his house.[54] He carried Pugin's bright polychromy to the medieval city of Bruges, doing what in many ways Pugin had wished he could have done himself, for one of Pugin's greatest disappointments was that he was not invited to do more work in a great medieval city such as Oxford.

Pugin visited France often and stayed in close touch with architectural developments there. The restoration of Sainte Chapelle in Paris, which was ongoing throughout his lifetime, influenced his own design work, but conversely his influence helped francophone designers see the potential of asymmetrical church planning.[55] George Gilbert Scott carried Puginian principles to Germany with his designs for Hamburg's Nikolaikirche, and later he sent them to Mumbai. In 1847, Pugin was awarded a gold medal by Pope Pius IX.

However, Pugin's success at popularising the Revival was not entirely to his benefit. Suddenly in the 1840s, architects of the archaeologically correct Gothic Revival seemed to be appearing everywhere. Pugin had competition. He also found that the polemical tone of much of his writing had offended many English Catholics and that some Anglican proponents of the Gothic cause, whom he would have expected to be his allies, were attacking him for his religion. In the mid-1840s, for the first time, major Catholic commissions began to go to other architects.

Southwark and Nottingham

In 1843, Pugin prepared a capriccio showing all of his church work to date, for the frontispiece of *An Apology for the Revival of Christian Architecture* (p 2). Capriccios of this type were popular among his contemporaries: the watercolourist John Gandy had prepared one of Soane's complete body of work, and C R Cockerell had produced a number of similar studies for his lectures as Professor of Architecture at the Royal Academy, showing famous buildings in comparative scale. Pugin created his capriccio in response to one of Cockerell's, engraved in 1841, that showed the churches of Christopher Wren. Pugin disliked Wren for using Classical temple forms. Typical of Pugin's sense of humour, he mimicked Cockerell's format to show how Christian churches should be built. He took liberties in portraying his own designs in their ideal states, with spires completed and, in some cases, with exaggerated scale. In pride of place at the centre of Pugin's etching was St George's, Southwark, begun in 1841 and destined to be London's first Roman Catholic Cathedral. It was to have been Pugin's largest church and should have been one of his proudest achievements.

Pugin designed it on the same formula as Cheadle, but magnified it for the scale of the world's largest metropolis. The aisles and nave were independently gabled in order to break up the mass. A very long nave, almost three times as long as it was wide, was to have terminated in a very tall tower at the west end.

Pugin had planned to spend his life at work on it. The cathedral was never finished, however, and was largely destroyed in the Second World War. Its ruins were incorporated into a new church in the 1950s. Although it was one of the most visible Catholic churches in England, the funds simply were not

Interior of St George's Cathedral, Southwark. [Public Domain]

St George's, Southwark, before it was damaged during the Second World War. [Historic England Archive CC97/00617]

St George's, Southwark, as Pugin intended it to look, drawn by Peter Anson in 1936. [© Historic England Archive ME001058]

St Barnabas' Cathedral, Nottingham. [Diocese of Nottingham]

available for a church of appropriate grandeur. The result was an embarrassment and a frustration for Pugin. It was perhaps the most disappointing of his large churches: the nave had a reputation for being narrow and tunnel-like and the outside walls were lined with short, fussy pinnacles.

However, Pugin was soon able to demonstrate what he could do with a cruciform cathedral church. At St Barnabas', Nottingham, which was commenced in 1842, his new ideas began to come through.

Pugin felt that his designs were constantly improving, and in what was a common refrain in his letters, he declared that St Barnabas' 'would be by far the richest thing attempted since the olden time ... 3 times the solemnity of St George's – or Birmingham'.[56] Rather than the overly long nave of St George's, the chancel and nave were closer in length, and the nave was built

45

Interior of St Barnabas' Cathedral, Nottingham. The encaustic tile pavement has since been restored. [Diocese of Nottingham]

with a 2:3 ratio of width to length, a proportion that he would stick to for the rest of his career.[57] From this point forward, rather than building as high as he could, Pugin brought ceiling heights down, keeping them in careful proportional relationship to the rest of the church – at St Giles', Cheadle, for instance, the nave height is equivalent to three-quarters of its length. Nottingham's central tower with chapels stacked up at the east end created a pyramidal composition rather than a linear one. The interior was Pugin's most complex, with cross views through screened arches, made possible by an ambulatory and transepts.

Pugin must have been pleased with the design, for he would repeat the use of screened chancel walls in his next large church, St Aidan's Cathedral, Enniscorthy. The interior of St Barnabas' was very plain in terms of ornament, with the exception of the Chapel of the Blessed Sacrament, which was richly painted in the manner of Cheadle and featured an elaborately carved ciborium over the altar, one of the most elaborate altar canopies Pugin ever created. The illustration of the interior and the text in *Present State* make clear that he had hoped that similar patterned decoration could eventually be added to the chancel.[58]

Late churches

In keeping with Lord Shrewsbury's wishes that the costs of building be kept in check, St Barnabas' exterior is also strikingly plain. The clustered chapels, chancel, and sacristy support each other, resulting in few buttresses or pinnacles, and clean rooflines. The contrast with the stumpy pinnacles of St George's makes it hard to believe that these churches were designed only a year apart. In his later years, Pugin began to be more restrained in his use of ornament. He became better at achieving desired effects economically – he was still learning as he went along and was, after all, only 30 when he designed St Barnabas'. That is not to say that his interiors ever ceased to be richly painted and patterned when he could arrange it. He was just more judicious in the use of such patterns. At the mortuary chapel of the Rolle family at Bicton, Devon, for instance, in which Pugin was clearly able to indulge his love of ornament, he left the carved stone walls unpainted, under a painted ceiling.

His late church interiors, even when very richly ornamented, did not pursue the intense colouration of Cheadle. He wrote in about 1845, 'something even grander than most of the old things can be produced by simplicity combined with gigantic proportions', a stance that would be echoed by later Gothic Revivalists such as Giles Gilbert Scott.[59]

He had written in *True Principles*, albeit with regard to domestic architecture, that symmetry for its own sake was a 'great error', the elevation should be '*made subservient to the plan*'.[60] In most cases, plans should be asymmetrical, responding to natural requirements of use. He first tried placing a tower at the end of an aisle at St Mary's, Stockton-on-Tees, in 1841. By 1843, he was placing towers to one side in all his churches, and making single-aisled plans. These two changes transformed the spatial experience of his buildings. The result was a space less focused on the procession down a central aisle to the altar. The sense of mystery was increased. Instead of presenting itself all at once, there were additional spaces to be explored and

Rolle Mortuary Chapel, Bicton. [© Historic England Archive AA98/04724]

revealed. This was a significant shift in spatial hierarchy, with the baptistries and chapels, the areas for private devotion, becoming destinations in their own right. Pugin had been feeling his way towards this arrangement from the beginning by screening these areas of the church, and now he had found an effective way to realise it.

Many medieval churches, of course, did have a tower symmetrically placed at the centre of the west end. But Pugin found that asymmetry best achieved his true principles. At St Peter's, Marlow, Buckinghamshire (1845–8), he made the tower and nave flush behind a taut skin of knapped flint, creating a box that breaks up into shapes that reveal its varying functions as the walls rise.

At St Marie's, Rugby (1846), and St Osmund's, Salisbury (1847–8), Pugin explored the principle of asymmetry at its most extreme. In both these unusual churches he placed the chancel off-centre.

St Peter's, Marlow. [© Mr A S Heywood-Jones/Historic England Archive IOE01/03765/31]

Ecclesiologists had noted the irregularities in some medieval churches and attributed significance to them, and here Pugin tried such an irregularity himself. The result is strikingly eccentric, but we do not know what Pugin was aiming for. As far as is known, he never wrote about it.

At St Marie's, Liverpool, Pugin explored the town church typology, designing a church with a clerestory to gather light from above the tops of tall surrounding buildings that otherwise might overshadow the church. The suggestion that churches in cities should be built differently from churches in the country would be championed by the architect G E Street. It became one of the key concepts of the High Victorian Gothic Revival. Pugin examined the problem of the urban church in his final book, *Treatise on Chancel Screens & Rood Lofts*, in 1851, a year after Street addressed the same issue in a letter to *The Ecclesiologist*.[61]

Because urban churches needed different strategies to allow for the circulation of large numbers of communicants, Pugin began to design them

St Osmund's, Salisbury. [© Mr Peter Read/Historic England Archive IOE01/14566/24]

St Mary's Cathedral, Newcastle. [© Historic England Archive DP058454]

Petre Chantry,
St George's
Cathedral,
Southwark.
[Britain Express]

with aisles on either side of the chancel. At St Mary's, Newcastle-upon-Tyne (1842–4), the chancel is not a separate projection from the body of the church, but the rear wall of the chancel is flush with the walls of the side chapels.

Instead, the chancel is signified by a dais. This allowed communicants easy egress from the altar via the side-aisles. Importantly, it also brought the seated congregation closer to the altar. This change is essential for understanding Pugin's late churches. His increasing concern with the congregation's ability to clearly see and experience the Mass, and his inclusion of features without medieval precedents, such as confessionals and glazed porches, marked a shift in his ecclesiology. He did not abandon Sarum Use, rather he designed churches that could also accommodate the Tridentine liturgies that were by far the most common form of modern Catholic worship.[62] Pugin had moved away from strict medievalism. In 1845, he wrote a letter to *The Builder* that contained a sentiment he would increasingly repeat during his final years: 'I have long entertained the sanguine hope that Christian art and architecture may be carried to a far higher degree of perfection than they ever attained in the middle ages'.[63]

Pugin was now more willing to stray from the strict Decorated Gothic features that the Revd Dr Rock and the Ecclesiologists had so strenuously promoted. Perhaps he began to abandon such inflexible interpretations around the time the Ecclesiologists began to criticise him and his friendship with Rock had cooled. For just as ancient Roman architectural practice seldom followed the rules of Vitruvius, so medieval designers seldom precisely followed the rules of Durandus or the Sarum Missal. Pugin began to draw more creatively from a wider range of precedents. The 1848 Petre Chantry in St George's is Perpendicular Gothic in style, complete with fan vaulting, a form of late Gothic he previously would have considered debased. Violating his true principles of exposed construction, the scissor-trussed roof of St Augustine, Ramsgate, was to have been panelled over.[64]

By the late 1840s, Pugin also seemed to be moving away from his obsession with the church as a symbolic text, easing up slightly on the intensity with which he had previously ascribed every space with an analogical meaning. His 1849 book *Floriated Ornament* made no mention of didactic ornament, but focused instead on the study of nature as the basis of ornamental form. Pugin describes himself picking up a dried thistle and discovering in it the perfect Gothic foliage. He mirrored Ruskin in claiming that 'It is impossible to improve on the works of God; and the natural outlines of leaves, flowers, &c. must be more perfect than any invention of man'.[65] In the 20th century, Frank Lloyd Wright would show a similar interest in the structure of dried weeds – surely a result of the Gothic Revival roots of his education.

St Augustine's, Ramsgate

Pugin's final masterpiece was his own church at Ramsgate, which he began in 1846.

The church was dedicated to St Augustine, who had landed nearby in the 6th century on a mission to bring the Celtic bishops back into the Roman fold. Pugin took Augustine as a special patron because they shared a name (Augustus), an affiliation with Kent, and a mission to return Britain to the authority of Rome. Pugin built the church on his own land, next to his house.

He was his own client and paid for it himself. As such, he boasted to his son Edward, 'I am giving you the best architectural lessons I can; watch the church, there will be not a single "true principle" broken'.[66] Here, Pugin would be able to build his ideal church, the last statement of the architectural ideas he held at the end of his career – a wondrous church of solid rock on the cliffs above the sea.

The interior of St Augustine's was dark and mysterious.

Pugin described it as 'a true old thing solid & solemn ... all stone inside – just like one of the old buildings, and a fine screen'.[67] Entering from an unremarkable door in a plain wall running along the street, worshippers passed through a cloister and into the church itself. The colour palette was restrained – the walls were lined with grey ashlar, and even the stained glass eschewed his usual primary-colour scheme for dark reds, blues, and greens interspersed with black and silver. Artefacts glistened behind screens – rather than a riot of pattern all around, the attention was drawn to the concentrated colour of reredos, statue, and altar. The massive font made for the Medieval Court at the Great Exhibition would eventually tower at the end of the south aisle, straight ahead on entry from the cloister. The chancel was on the left. The overall impression was one of solidity – the banded flint exterior, the ashlar walls inside, the hard encaustic floor.

St Augustine's, Ramsgate. [Author]

The flints were a natural geological product of the chalk cliffs and were found in great profusion in the local area. The regional tradition of building with them dated to well before the Norman Conquest and, as Pugin would have known, St Augustine had used them to build his monastery.[68] Pugin had the edges all knapped so that the rough black edges glittered, an opulent treatment that contrasted with the plain brick of his house next door.

The plan was unusual – completely asymmetrical; there was one transept (which housed the Pugin chantry), one aisle (for accessing the chapels and baptismal font), and a central tower. The effect was to create multiple views through arches and screens, in a way that was more complex even than St Barnabas', Nottingham. Movement was across, as well as along the primary axes – the nave had to be traversed diagonally to reach the font, the chantry, or the confessionals. Just as Cheadle had been, the church would be visited by architectural pilgrims, from George Gilbert Scott to Norman Shaw. The High Victorian Gothic was beginning to emerge – complete with its eclecticism, muscularity, and prioritising of atmospheric effect. Once again, Pugin was spurring a revolution in church architecture. However, it was not only church architecture that Pugin had set out to transform. His aim had been to renew British Society in its entirety, and now we will turn to his other revolution: the transformation of house design.

Interior of St Augustine's, Ramsgate. [Historic England Archive CC43/00022]

2 The house of man

In 1835, a curious structure was built near the banks of the River Avon on the outskirts of Salisbury. It might easily have been mistaken for a garden folly belonging to nearby Clarendon Park, but in fact it was the eccentric house of Augustus Pugin.

The house, which he named St Marie's Grange, was his first constructed building, and as such announced a career shift from furniture maker and Covent Garden set designer to architect and decorator. He wrote excitedly to his friend Edward James Wilson, urging him to visit: 'the great thickness of the walls 3 f[eet], the approach over a drawbridge, the chapel with its little belfry – the antient letters worked in bricks in the walls, the gilt vanes on the roof – and the small windows all have astonished people here beyond measure'.[1] He continued in a second letter, 'I will put you in a bed room of the most solemn appearance. Fine old damask. Stone chimney oak furniture … You have no idea how compleat my house is'.[2] The locals had good reason to be astonished, for it was the first house to be built in Britain using medieval principles of planning and construction in several hundred years.

The house was tall and narrow, almost a tower, built of brick with stone trim, and capped with high-pitched roofs. The arriving visitor had to climb a staircase set into the hillside, cross a drawbridge, pass through a studded oak front door onto the landing of a spiral staircase, and go from there into the parlour. In reality, though, the house was small. The first floor contained three principal rooms arranged in an L-shaped plan: beyond the parlour was a library and a double-height chapel.

The ground floor contained a kitchen, scullery, and maid's room. The second floor housed two bedrooms. A garderobe tower provided a toilet on each floor. There were no corridors, and the only way to move through the house was via the spiral staircase and then by passing from room to room. What Pugin did not mention in his letter to Wilson was that because there were no corridors, the Pugins and their two children would have to pass through his bedroom anytime they needed to access the stairs.

In theory, the plan was a considered an attack on the carefully guarded privacy of the typical Regency house. Pugin believed the house was the seat

Watercolours of St Marie's Grange as it appeared when Pugin lived there. [RIBA Collections RIBA13245]

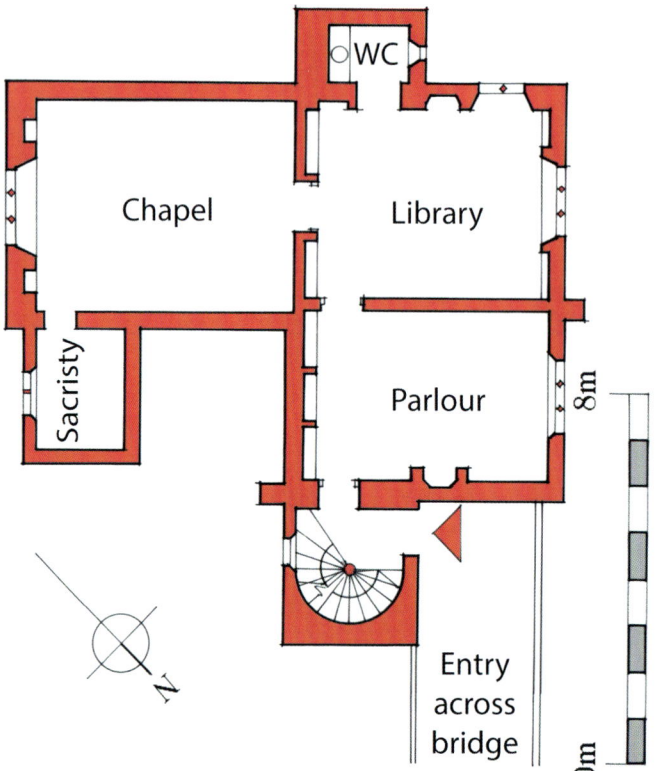

Plan of St Marie's Grange. [Timothy Brittain-Catlin]

of the owner's household in the 'Jolly Olde England' sense, and as such was the setting in which the individual would enact the Christian mandates of hospitality and charity. The sharing of spaces was meant to encourage bonhomie and egalitarianism as it did on a ship at sea. He would continue to develop that aspect of medieval domesticity in his later house designs.

However, at St Marie's Grange he did not quite have it right. When his wife became pregnant with his second daughter, Agnes, she found it was impossible to avoid the need to climb up and down the spiral staircase, and there was no privacy from children or servants or guests. Although the intention was egalitarian, it must have been awkward for all parties. Less than two years after moving in, the Pugins abruptly gave up the house and rented lodgings in Chelsea.[3]

St Marie's Grange sat empty for over three years; its eccentricity made it unsaleable. Therefore in 1841, a clever alteration was made to make the house more liveable – a rectangular staircase hall was inserted in the crook of the L. Most major rooms opened directly into this hall, solving the privacy issue, and the stair provided a more commodious way to move between levels. Scholars have long assumed that Pugin made these changes himself, because the inclusion of such a stair hall became the favoured solution in his later houses for joining medieval design with Victorian needs.[4] Pugin was rumoured to have spent more than £2,000 building St Marie's Grange, and in the end he sold it for £500 to the man from whom he had bought the land.[5]

Father of the Victorian villa

Is it possible that this somewhat unsuccessful experiment in medieval living was, as many claim, the seed from which the typical Victorian villa was born? Could St Marie's Grange really be the ancestor of the ranks of brick Gothic gables amidst crunching gravel paths that surround British towns from Bournemouth to Belfast? In a way, it was. For here, already, the features that would mark Pugin's mature domestic work were beginning to appear.

Watercolour showing the interior of St Marie's Grange during Pugin's occupancy. [Public Domain]

The revolutionary aspects of his work that would prove so popular included asymmetry – houses whose plans reflect household needs and whose façades were expressions of use. In the case of suburban villas, this meant giving prominence to the drawing room and main bedroom with a bay window. A corollary to this was the abolition of front and back. Pugin despised the 'stuck on Gothic fronts' of what he termed 'street-door residences'.[6] Instead he treated his house designs as fully three-dimensional objects. Construction also mattered. Instead of the stuccoed fronts of the Regency, it was important to Pugin that houses be solidly built and expressive of their structure. And finally, architectural space was made romantic and theatrical. Houses were to be travelled through and experienced: the stone Gothic columns on the vine-embowered porch, the encaustic tiled hall with arched corridor beyond (often leading to nowhere but a scullery), stained glass on the staircase and in the transom, all of these Victorian features were encouraged by Pugin's example. St Marie's Grange, though it was not yet a perfect expression of those things, marked their first appearance in the world, and as such, it was an earthquake of a house.

Despite its inconveniences, it must have been a beautiful building. The house as it stands today has been extensively modified – incredibly most doors have been moved, new bay windows punched through, old windows blocked up, ceilings covered, additions built. It is difficult to visualise Pugin's original house from what remains. However, one Pugin watercolour gives us a sense of what the interiors must have been like.

It shows the view from the library through to the chapel. Pugin's books fill the shelves, framed prints hang around the carved stone doorframe through which are seen the traceried chapel window and furnished altar. A Latin motto is painted in a frieze under the beamed ceiling. The effect is simple and stately.

Pugin's library

The presence of the library itself signals something crucial about Pugin's architectural practice. St Marie's Grange was small, without even a dining room. (Where the family took their meals is something of a mystery.) And yet Pugin considered both library and chapel to be essentials. The library was Pugin's workspace. Pugin sought to rediscover a lost system of design, and thus needed access to precedents and ideas. His work depended on the thorough study of medieval sources, both in artefact form and in print. His collections included prints by artists such as Wenceslaus Hollar showing pre-industrial architecture and cityscapes.

He had images of chalices and candlesticks, and numerous prints with religious subjects – particularly by Albrecht Dürer, whose work he greatly admired.

View of Greenwich by Wenceslaus Hollar, which Phoebe Stanton believed could be seen hanging in Pugin's library on p 59. [Public Domain]

Pugin's book and print collection was not merely an image library. He was well read in history, arts, and liturgy, declaring 'The history of architecture is the history of the world'.[7] The understanding of liturgy, especially, was central to his own faith and to his church work, and he eventually owned over 60 volumes on the subject.[8] As a professor at Oscott, he was able to converse and correspond with scholars and theologians from across Britain and Europe. 'I am a builder-up of men's minds and ideas as well as material edifices', he wrote, 'and there is an immense work and a moral foundation yet required before they are prepared to receive, understand, and practically realise the glories of Christian art'.[9]

In terms of his design work, the purpose of studying precedents was not to select details to copy, but to better understand a system and to find solutions for architectural problems. 'Nothing can be more dangerous', he warned, 'than looking at prints or buildings and trying to imitate bits of them'.[10] Seeking the spirit, not the letter, of medieval design became part of the rubric of the Gothic Revival, propounded not just by Pugin's successors in the mid-19th century, but by Giles Gilbert Scott in the mid-20th and Stephen Dykes Bower, whose works were still being constructed in the 21st. It also became the chief justification for the revival of handicrafts, so that the living artist could infuse his or her work with a unique spirit, but that was after Pugin's lifetime.

Bishop's House, Birmingham

Pugin began to develop ideas from St Marie's Grange at the Bishop's House he built next to St Chad's Cathedral in 1840.

The building was intended to house the Roman Catholic Bishop and his deputies, and its first occupant was Bishop Thomas Walsh, Vicar Apostolic of the Central District, whose initials Pugin incorporated into the brickwork.[11]

Bishop's House, Birmingham, as illustrated by Pugin in *The Present State of Ecclesiastical Architecture.* [Public Domain]

Plan of Bishop's House, Birmingham. [Timothy Brittain-Catlin]

Court

0m   8m

Great
Hall

Audience
Chamber

Bedroom

Bedroom

Chapel   Library   Chamber

A tall, urban courtyard house with hard industrial brick edges, the building was a crystalline composition of rectangular volumes. The plan was U-shaped, with the open side of the U forming the primary street-front.

Two tall gabled ends were connected by a low ground-floor passage that shielded the view of the central courtyard from the street. When standing near the cathedral, a stair turret with a pyramidal roof could be seen rising up inside the courtyard, and the roofline of the house terminated in wide rectangular chimneys that projected slightly from the walls. The windows

Great hall of the Bishop's House. [© Historic England Archive AA58/04264]

were mostly pointed lancets set with plate-glass sashes. Major rooms, such as the bishop's sitting room, were marked with bay windows; the two most important rooms, the chapel and the hall, were marked with traceried lights. Pugin explained, 'the elevation has been left in that natural irregularity produced by internal arrangements, to which we owe the picturesque effect of ancient buildings'.[12] Tall, riveting, and strange, the building looks most powerful in black and white photographs, with slightly soot-streaked walls and a Ford Anglia parked in front.

When describing the Bishop's House in *The Present State of Ecclesiastical Architecture in England* (hereafter *Present State*), Pugin explained that ecclesiastical residences should exhibit 'a solid, solemn, and scholastic character, that bespoke them at once to be the habitations of men who were removed far beyond the ordinary pursuits of life'.[13] The austerity of the house reflected its purpose – the building itself should be a devotional aid, shielding its residents from temptations and, through the use of judiciously placed symbolic ornament, encouraging them to keep their minds on God. The lack of ostentation, it was hoped, would also make it more welcoming for poor parishioners. Rather than the bishop's private domain, a palace where one of the Lords Spiritual might live like a lord of the manor, Pugin envisaged the Bishop's House as a place of hospitality. There were eight bedrooms in the attic 'for strangers', and the great hall could seat 60 for a meal.

It was an emphatically psychological way of conceiving a house. Rather than simply providing shelter, Pugin's domestic designs were intended to constantly coax and encourage certain behaviours in their occupants. It was a way of thinking about houses conceived for the 19th century. Pugin wrote that in the absence of a fully Catholic society, the building itself could help to provide support for the cleric's purpose:

> Our catholic ancestors … knew devotion in the sanctuary was only to be obtained by gravity and solemnity without … and this would not have been possible for them to perform had they not resided in the solemn and retired structures provided for them. But if such edifices were found necessary for the promotion of regularity and discipline in the days of faith, and in times when the clergy had such vast resources in mutual support, how much more are they required amongst us at the present time, when our ecclesiastics are scattered in populous towns, frequently alone and unsupported, and where almost every spot, except their own domain, is poisoned with heresy, infidelity, and licentiousness![14]

Pugin was keen to emphasise, however, that a lack of ornament was not the same as a lack of basic comfort. The houses of the Middle Ages had been comfortable in themselves, he claimed, and with the addition of 19th-century technology a Gothic house should be as cosy as any other.[15] And whereas St Marie's Grange had no corridors, the Bishop's House had as many as possible. Corridors became a vehicle in Pugin's architecture for creating drama in a space. At the Bishop's House, instead of providing a staircase leading directly from the entrance to the great hall, corridors guide the visitor around the entire perimeter of the courtyard, creating the longest circulation route possible and carrying the visitor through a series of different corridor types and changes of level. Not only could corridors create anticipation and a sense of approach, but their receding arches, ceiling beams, and rows of windows could create picturesque views and spatial complexity.[16]

Library of Taymouth Castle. [James Brittain/Country Life Picture Library]

Pugin as decorator

Making use of the picturesque potential of circulation space was a way that Pugin's work differed from its Georgian predecessors and was one of his legacies to the Victorian villa. His eye for the theatrical may have come from his days as a set designer. Although his decorative work changed as he matured, the theatricality always remained. His early library at Taymouth Castle, Perthshire, designed in 1837, was dripping with pinnacles, tracery, and fretwork, every surface minutely carved, as if Oxford's Divinity School had been shrunk, gilded, and filled with parlour furniture.

At Lismore Castle, County Waterford, one of his last, designed around 1851, he provided the great hall with a large brass Hardman chandelier, linenfold panelling, and a trussed ceiling stencilled with gold stars.

Great hall, Lismore Castle. [Jonathan Gibson/Country Life Picture Library]

Throughout his career, Pugin worked as a designer of fashionable residential interiors, mostly for large country houses. He often carried out this work in association with someone else – sometimes an architect such as Gillespie Graham, or at other times a firm of London decorators such as J G Crace and Company. On rare occasions, such as with his work at Alton Towers or Scarisbrick Hall, he was commissioned directly. Such collaborations could vary in scope, from Pugin merely supplying designs for a fireplace and leaving the details to be filled in by his collaborators, to complete schemes for fitting and furnishing whole rooms including panelling and structural beams. The process usually worked this way: Pugin

Pugin's drawings of a corridor and the kitchen at Scarisbrick Hall. [© Historic England Archive CC000391]

was supplied with measurements without having seen the house in person, and he returned drawings via post, receiving a cheque in return. If the job were more elaborate, he might make a visit to the site to oversee installation or to order corrections to the workmanship. In many cases the clients had no direct dealings with Pugin at all.

In his country house work, Pugin was designing for existing buildings, many of which, including Alton Towers, Scarisbrick Hall, and Bilton Grange, had been Gothicised earlier in the century in a way he found displeasing. He therefore often added features to disguise flat façades or disrupt symmetry. These were country houses with long traditions of additive construction, and they continued to develop after Pugin had departed. His greatest contribution to the country house genre was the first full-blown revived medieval great hall, which he built as Lord Shrewsbury's dining room at Alton Towers in 1836.[17] He felt that great halls were essential to the revival of Christian hospitality in the large household, and he would add them to a number of country houses. He sometimes found clever solutions to architectural problems at the houses he was called to work on, such as at Scarisbrick Hall, where he designed two long corridors, one on top of the other, and made the ceiling of the bottom corridor open along the sides in order to borrow daylight from the corridor above. The floor of the top corridor thus essentially became a long bridge resting on beams, an arrangement he might have seen in the walkways of ships.

At Scarisbrick, he also designed a great hall and a clocktower.

Scarisbrick Hall, south elevation. [© Historic England Archive CC000388]

One of the elaborate interiors Pugin created for Scarisbrick Hall. [© Historic England Archive DP033749]

He made the house appear picturesquely irregular in the way he advocated in his writings, and he applied new and better detailing to the existing house. Here he hoped to build his ideal Catholic mansion, but his client, as much as Pugin admired him, was not a great medieval lord, but the somewhat reclusive collector, Charles Scarisbrick, seeking a romantic setting to display his collections. His work at Scarisbrick was essentially a cosmetic treatment.

He certainly had ideas about how he would design a country house from scratch, illustrating the ideal 'Old English Catholic mansion' in *True Principles* and designing an unexecuted moated country manor in Leicestershire for his patron Ambrose Phillips, but he was never commissioned to actually build one.

For many houses, Pugin designed a wide range of fittings and furnishings. There were Gothic doorknobs, brass chandeliers with spiralling metal foliage, and wallpapers patterned after damask hangings. Heraldic motifs often formed a basis for the colour scheme and provided a programme of unified ornament.

He designed so much of each room not because he wanted to express a personal artistic vision; this was not *gesamtkunstwerk*, seeking total immersion in a personal Augustus Pugin style. Instead, he designed many details because he was concerned with making a room truly Gothic. Because few suitable Gothic items were available, he often had to design everything himself. He was happy to use designs by others when they met his principles.

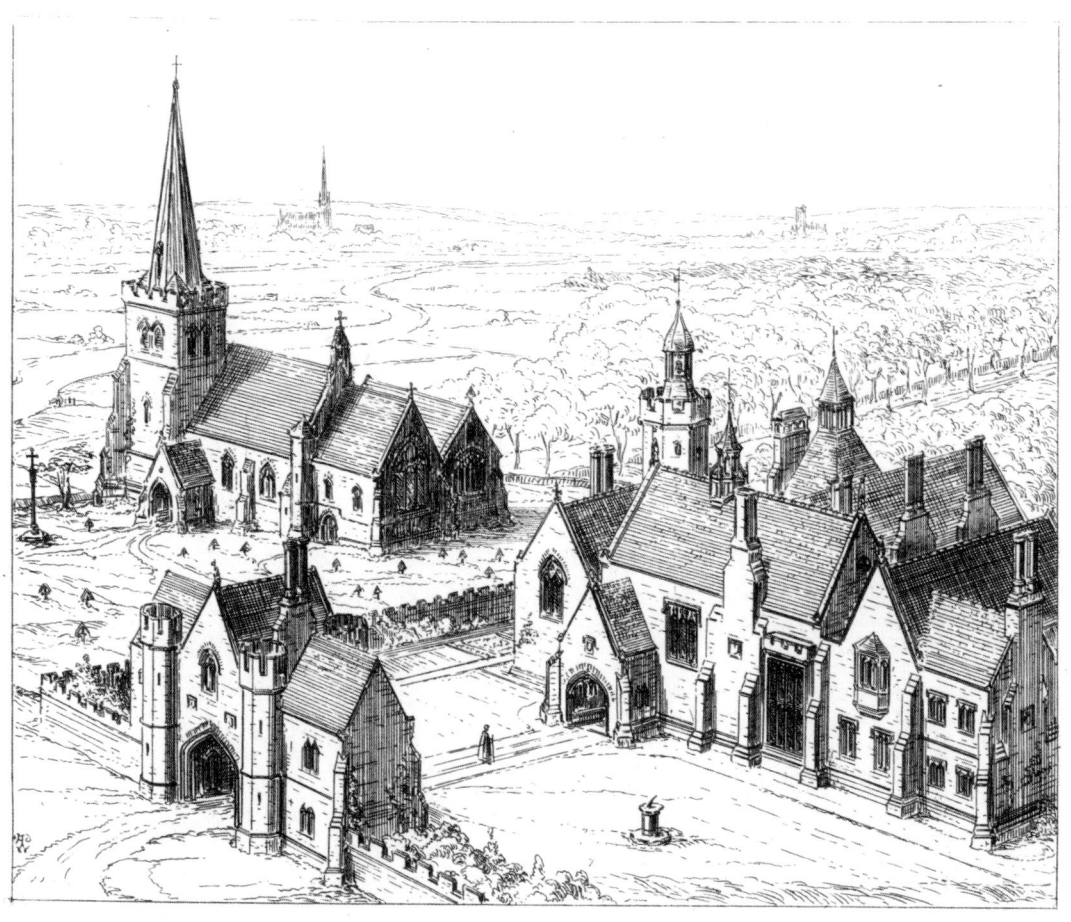

An ideal house, as illustrated in *True Principles*. [Public Domain]

Genuine medieval objects were always welcome, but also creations of other Victorian designers, such as the off-the-peg wallpaper that he used in the back corridors of The Grange at Ramsgate.[18] What mattered was stylistic consistency, because it implied a coherent system of ideas.

The typical Pugin interior featured dark, wood panelling and boldly coloured and patterned wallpaper densely hung with pictures, furniture with ornamental detail in carved, dark wood, glistening metalwork, and stained glass.[19] For many of Pugin's clients, these rooms provided settings in which to display their art collections. This cluttering with treasures, of course, was not medieval, but a legacy of Horace Walpole's Gothick and the Romantic Movement.[20] No medieval merchant's house would have been filled with church paintings or have been decorated with wallpaper. For many of his clients, their art collections were not even primarily medieval. His patron at Scarisbrick, for instance, mostly collected 17th-century Dutch paintings and owned 24 canvases by Benjamin West.[21] Pugin was also willing to continue the Regency trend of using turned-chairs (with rectangular back pads and spiral legs) to furnish Gothic interiors, even though they were the product of a later era.[22] As in his days at Covent Garden, what mattered was atmosphere.

The sale of artworks and the modernist fashion for measured spacing of objects have altered most surviving Pugin interiors. Besides St Mary's College, Oscott, and the House of Lords, very few Pugin interiors retain a significant amount of their original furniture. None of his residential interiors retain their furniture or the collections of medieval art they were designed to house. The growing appreciation of medieval art that Pugin himself worked so hard to foster meant that the value of such artwork in these collections skyrocketed, even within his clients' lifetimes. Some of the objects collected by Pugin and his patrons are now in the collections of the Victoria and Albert Museum and the Metropolitan Museum of Art. The rise of interest in Victorian art in the last decades of the 20th century has led to much Pugin-designed furniture also ending up in private collections or the galleries of museums. If we wish to understand these interiors the way Pugin meant for them to be experienced, then we must imagine their original appearance.

Pugin's most resplendent country house interiors could not present more of a contrast with the stark simplicity he advocated in *True Principles*. Had he not written of the impropriety of a residence being decorated with the grandeur of a church, and that dense ornament should never be applied

Wallpaper designed by Pugin for Magdalen College, Oxford. [© Victoria and Albert Museum, London]

simply for the sake of decoration?[23] And yet in practice he seemed content to supply fittings, a fireplace, and stencilled patterns for a ceiling, for instance, with the rest of the detail to be filled in by a collaborator, even to the point of sham construction or furniture that violated his principles. William Morris was deeply torn over the fact that, in his own case, he promoted a socialist movement to revive handicraft, a movement intended to equalise social differences and to enrich the lives of everyday people, and yet made his living 'ministering to the swinish luxury of the rich'.[24] Pugin faced a similar predicament, but did not find it as soul-wrenching. He occasionally pleaded with Lord Shrewsbury to let him rebuild Alton Towers in accordance with his principles, and he once wrote to a collaborator, the decorator J G Crace, asking if they should not be doing more simple, affordable, structural Gothic furniture in order to spread the taste for Gothic among the middle class.[25] However, he was more of an optimist and more of a pragmatist than Morris. For Pugin, any 'correctly' detailed Gothic fireplace, any new canonically correct lamb and flag stencil was, as he used to say when he completed drawings, 'so much to the good'.[26] He stood upon the rock of his faith, and he believed that every bit of Gothic design he could produce was an instrument of God's work.

Much of Pugin's architectural career was devoted to decoration. Once again unity was key. Pugin did not think of decoration as a separate design task: Christian art was Christian art, regardless of the scale of the work. Architecture was a framework for furnishings and decoration and had to exist in symbiosis with it. The artist-decorator model that he pioneered, in which an architect or designer worked closely with manufacturers to produce the decorative arts that would complete their architectural work, would form an essential element of Arts and Crafts design practice and would set the standard for later firms such as Morris & Co. and Watts & Co.

The Grange

In 1844, atop a chalk cliff overlooking the English Channel at Ramsgate, Pugin built a new house for himself. He named it The Grange.

Apparently he felt that the medieval term grange, referring to a small manor house with rambling farm buildings, was the closest medieval parallel for his modern suburban house. Pugin would spend the second half of his architectural career at this new grange. Ramsgate was a place he knew and loved. He had gone there with his aunt as a young man, and the region, known in the Middle Ages as the Isle of Thanet, had a rich Christian history. St Augustine, a saint with whom Pugin shared a name and felt a special connection, had landed nearby and founded the cathedral of Canterbury, mother church of English Christianity, a few miles inland. Pugin could just see the silhouette of the cathedral from the tower of his new house. There

The Grange, Ramsgate. [Author]

were a number of medieval knapped flint churches in the area, and Pugin celebrated their presence in a stained-glass map set into one of the drawing room windows. The train could carry him to London in a few hours, or if he preferred, he could go by steamship. The town itself was a popular sea resort as well as a port. The small local Catholic community was often augmented by the presence of Catholic sailors.

From the top of the tower, using one of the brass telescopes he kept in a rack in the entry hall, he could watch the ships, and beyond he could see France, the land of his father's birth. If any of the ships became stranded on the sands, Pugin could sound the alarm and rush down the stairs and into the tunnel he had cut through the cliff from his house to his sloop, *Caroline*, on the beach below. He and his crew would rescue whatever sailors and cargo they could. The tunnel also provided convenient cover, locals whispered, so that he could avoid paying duties on medieval artefacts smuggled from the Continent.

The Grange was a thoroughly maritime house. Sometimes a sudden gust of sea breeze would rush through the interior when all the windows and doors were closed, confirming the presence of the tunnel below. The banner with Pugin's martlet emblem flapping atop the tower was visible from the sea and used by sailors as a landmark. Pugin wore sailor's clothes throughout his life, and kept his house 'ship-shape', insisting that everything be neatly tucked away in its proper place at the end of the day, not even relaxing this rule on Christmas Day.[27] He installed plate glass windows to take best advantage of the sea views – which also, incidentally, gave the best light for drawing.

When he had first decided to build The Grange, Pugin bought a good-sized parcel of land on the edge of the growing town, and from the beginning he planned a small church, priest's house, cemetery, and chantry chapel next to the house.

Here too, as at Birmingham, Cheadle, and Alton, he was creating a little world, rebuilding Catholic England half an acre at a time. At The Grange, the

Watercolour birds-eye view of the Grange and St Augustine's, Ramsgate.
[Private Collection]

Office was read for the household several times a day in the private chapel, with Pugin acting as cantor, accompanied by his daughter Anne on the pedal organ. Even before the church was ready for use, Pugin would sometimes provide services for the Thanet Catholic community on the grounds of his house.[28]

The Grange was well-known from the first. Built at the height of Pugin's career, it was widely published and even shown in bird's-eye view at the Royal Academy. Like Cheadle, it attracted a stream of architectural pilgrims. Sightseers wanting to see the famous house eventually become an annoyance for Pugin, who ordered that they should not be admitted. The house was the heart that would pump the blood of Pugin's domestic principles into the suburbs and villages of Britain. It was his domestic manifesto – a built example of the ideal family house.

Construction and defence

Like St Marie's Grange nine years before, The Grange was built of brick with stone dressings. The main body of the house was two storeys with attics, a square tower rising above. Its masses did not ramble and, combined with Pugin's dislike of horizontal stringcourses, this meant it felt compact. The plain brick skin, lack of ornament, and varying window types gave it a sense of Tudor modesty. Pugin walled off the property with a high brick wall, and entrance was through a small gate on an alley rather than directly from the main road. Visitors passed through this gate into a courtyard situated between the road and the house and surrounded with low brick buildings including a 'cartoon room' for the production of large stained-glass cartoons that by this point made up a significant portion of Pugin's business. Ahead, there was a house for a resident priest. The Grange itself was on the right side, and one had to move into the courtyard to see the entry door concealed at the centre of the west façade. Approaching the door, one would find that although there was a knocker and a bell-pull, there was no doorknob – the braced and studded oak door could only be opened from the inside. Although not overly large, the house's construction was massive, with a high-water table in battered brick. The Grange did not have any of the trappings of defence – there was no drawbridge this time, and certainly no arrow slits or machicolations – but it felt strong. 'I shall not erect a grecian villa', Pugin wrote, 'but a substantial catholic house not large but convenient & solid'.[29]

Pugin was disparaging of mock castles; the trappings of the medieval military, he felt, were ridiculous in a modern house.[30] A modern castle was nonsense, he wrote, because the castle form did not relate in any way to modern needs. No house needed to withstand a siege or repel an army. Besides, 19th-century castles were seldom actually defensible, and although they featured imposing fronts, 'round the corner of the building [there was probably] a conservatory leading to the principal rooms, through which a whole company of horsemen might penetrate at one smash to the heart of the mansion!'[31] He was distressed when Lord Shrewsbury asked him to rebuild the ruined castle at Alton, suggesting it could serve as a home for elderly priests: 'After writing a book against mock Castles, a book dedicated to your Lordship, you call on me to violate every principle and build a Castle *for Priests!!!!*'[32] Yet he eventually gave in and oversaw the rebuilding. The design was picturesque with a lookout turret, a high, leaded spire, and a tall, narrow chapel with a green-and-yellow-tiled roof built directly atop the ruined 13th-century crypt. Alton Castle was a fantasy, a theatrical plaything for the Earl, rather than an attempt at a strictly 'archaeologically correct' reconstruction of the historic castle, but the result at least adhered to a logic of defensibility.

Although he eschewed castle forms in houses, Pugin did feel the need for a certain level of fortification against the real dangers of the modern world – notably burglars, of which he had a great terror, and anti-Catholic riots. There never were any such riots in Ramsgate, but there nearly were in 1850, and Pugin's house and church would have been prime targets. In addition to only being approachable on foot through a gate and having no external doorknob on the main door, the ground-floor windows were divided by stone mullions and protected by massive internal shutters, each weighing 88kg.[33] The same walled perimeter and small windows appeared in the Bishop's House in Birmingham. St Marie's Grange, of course, had a drawbridge.

The thick walls of The Grange were not only defensive. Quality of construction was important to Pugin – in fact, essential. Without integrity of construction, a building could not be truly Gothic. Proper Gothic, he explained, was by definition 'bold and scientific construction ... light, and at the same time solid'.[34] In contrast to what he considered the gimcrack stucco fronts of John Nash's Regent's Park houses, it was built to last. And unlike Mediterranean villa forms, it was designed for the English climate: high-pitched roofs shed rain and snow; thick walls protected against cold and damp. It was surprisingly important to Pugin that his buildings be appropriate to the climate, even when it meant sacrificing authentic medieval features. When he designed an unexecuted residence for Bishop Wilson in Tasmania, he proposed a Gothic house with verandahs, a lightweight feature seemingly at odds with the Gothic solidity of the house, but that would protect the windows from solar gain and help to catch the breeze during hot Australian summers. Today, we would call his concern with a building's lifespan and climatic appropriateness sustainability. For Pugin, it was simply pragmatism and common sense.

Later Victorian architects would wrestle with the theme of natural science in their work, with William Butterfield evoking geologic time in the stratified walls of his churches, and Deane & Woodward responding to Darwin's idea of evolution in a wide range of naturalistic motifs in decoration, such as the typological iron foliage of the Oxford Museum.[35] Pugin did not think in that way. The Victorian project to organise scientific knowledge was far from Pugin's mind. His own respect for nature was more a product of the Romantic Movement – he valued local scenery and weather, the way the structures of Man added picturesque focal points to the landscape, and the way the weathering of natural materials aesthetically joined the two.

Banishing the box

The final great breakthrough at The Grange was its plan.

The house was designed on a pinwheel plan, which means that the main rooms were placed at 90-degree angles to one another, radiating off a central space to form a shape somewhat like a pinwheel. At the centre of the

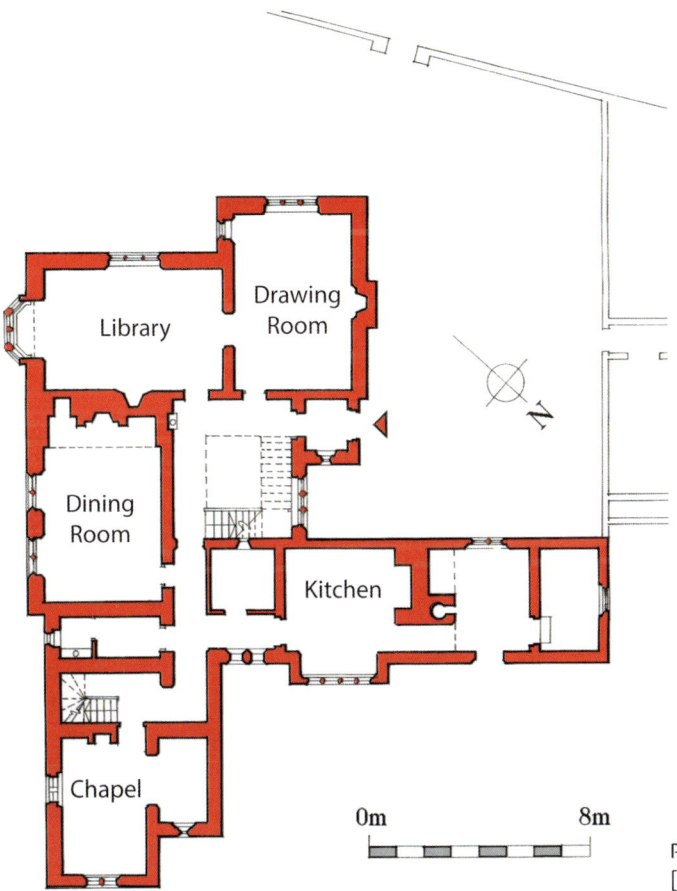

Plan of the Grange.
[Timothy Brittain-Catlin]

79

The upper staircase hall at the Grange, showing the pinwheel shape in the bannisters. [Author]

house was a two-storey stair hall, the innovation Pugin had hit on when he renovated St Marie's Grange.

All the major rooms, both upstairs and downstairs, opened into this hall. To the right of the ground-floor entrance was the rectangular drawing room, its short side opening into the stair hall. Turned 90 degrees so that its short side opened into the drawing room was the library, which projected out towards the sea. Another 90-degree turn made the dining room, running along the sea front of the house, and then another turn created the service wing containing the kitchen. Although others had used this plan type, Pugin seems to have been the first to recognise its potential for allowing each room of the house to take on an independent character and express itself externally. The last vestiges of the symmetrical format of Palladian planning were thus cast away. In keeping with his principles, the rooms were 'not masked or concealed under one monotonous front, but by their variety in form and outline increas[ed] the effect of the building'.[36]

Pugin's library at the Grange. [Author]

Different rooms were expressed externally with different window types – the location of the desk where Pugin worked in his library, for instance, was marked by a bay window facing the sea.

The variety of the façade was brought together as a unified composition by a consistent roofline. Thus every room could best meet the requirements of its use while maintaining a sense of order. Internally, moving through the house meant frequent turning, revealing new vistas each time. It gave the house a visual interest and made it seem larger. The visitor to The Grange was filled with a sense of exploration and discovery, as if it were a country house writ small. The pinwheel plan was the essential architectural concept of The Grange, its *parti pris*, and Pugin celebrated this fact by using a pinwheel motif in the bannisters of the central staircase.[37] On entering the house, pinwheel shapes thus spiralled up and around the visitor.

Rampisham Rectory. [Paul Barker/Country Life Picture Library]

The disadvantage of the pinwheel plan was a lack of privacy. It was considerably better than St Marie's Grange, but the bedroom doors were visible from the entrance hall, and Pugin's egalitarianism still prevailed, with servants, visitors, and family all crossing the central circulation space. Noise also travelled throughout the house, and even Pugin's nerves were sometimes frayed by the slamming doors and shouting voices of his six children echoing across the stair hall. He installed a curtain rather than a door between the library and the drawing room because 'a door once made is bound to be opened and slammed'.[38] The stair hall became a popular feature of English houses. Few, however, imitated Pugin's placement at the centre of the house. The pinwheel plan was not an aspect of The Grange that became widespread. The Victorians were increasingly tending towards separate service areas and elaborate arrangements for privacy and, as a result, later Victorians such as Charles Eastlake, found the plan of The Grange somewhat impractical.[39] Pugin liked it though, and he used it in the rest of his major houses, most notably Oswaldcroft in Liverpool, and the loveliest of his parsonages, the rectory of Rampisham, Dorset.

A Victorian ideal

When developing his domestic architecture, Pugin had looked to medieval precedents: the asymmetrical façade of Great Chalfield Manor, Wiltshire; the carved fireplaces and beamed ceilings of the surviving prior's lodgings at Muchelney, Somerset, and Wenlock, Shropshire; the kitchen of Glastonbury; the Jew's House in Lincoln; the bishop's palaces and surviving medieval houses of the cathedral cities. His study of the medieval house was as intensive as his study of the medieval church. The result, however, was not the rebirth of medieval house design. Rather, he had mined these houses for useful concepts. He fused the solidity and asymmetricality of Gothic building, to name just two characteristics, with modern technologies such as gas lighting, running water, and plate glass, with modern ways of decorating, and with new plan forms. The result was the medieval made modern.

The Grange, he felt, was a nearly ideal house. He wrote to his friend J R Bloxam of 'the delight of the sea with catholic architecture & a Library' and to Lord Shrewsbury: 'The Sea Brezze constantly blowing is delicious. the Garden is all Roses and Honeysuckles. a delightful perfume, brass bedstead with a Mattrass – every possible inducement'.[40] By uniting the modern and the Gothic, he had created something he felt was the best of all worlds.

The Chapel

JESUS COLLEGE

alte 1628

3   The seat of wisdom

On any given Sunday in 1850, John Sutton could be found playing a small organ in the medieval chapel of Jesus College, Cambridge. The boys' choir he had founded sang below, surrounded by members of the college community seated in Gothic stalls. Angels painted on the organ shutters held instruments and scrolls with the musical notation of the *Te Deum*, visually marking the space with the Gregorian chant that comprised its contemporary soundscape. The floor was paved with encaustic tile and white marble, the chancel was wrapped in coved screens carved with tracery and brattishing that ran between the medieval arches. Above the communion table, three pointed lancets shone with Hardman glass. It was a perfect vision of the medieval traditions of a 15th-century collegiate foundation. Except that, like most colleges of Britain's ancient universities, the so-called medieval traditions were recent rediscoveries or sympathetic new inventions. Only a few years previously, the chapel had featured a plaster ceiling, and a gallery that separated the fellows from the students.

The medieval arches had been blocked up, and there was no singing at all, except when the college paid a travelling choir, usually on three Sundays per year.[1] Pugin's transformation of the space had reprogrammed the institution.

The weekly routine of the college was renewed: its community worship ritualised; its musical life invigorated, setting the stage for the system of organ scholars and choral evensongs that define the Oxbridge colleges today. Not everyone in the mid-19th century may have wanted this transformation, but wanted or not, there was no denying that architectural change had compelled a change in the daily life of the college itself.

Pugin did a large amount of work for institutions – colleges, seminaries, convents, abbeys and priories. These building types are best examined as a group, because Pugin saw them as closely related. They all housed Christian communities that were engines of evangelisation, equipping their occupants and sending them out to spread the Gospel. They also shared a common architectural programme born out of a shared origin in the quadrangular cloister of medieval monasteries. They were all naturally groups of buildings organised around a courtyard or courtyards, with a need for

The Chapel at Jesus College, Cambridge, before Pugin's alterations. [Jesus College Archives]

Jesus College Chapel as it appeared after Pugin's alterations, as shown in a photograph from 1908. [Jesus College Archives]

chapel, refectory, kitchen, residential accommodation and, usually, a library. Building these institutions provided an opportunity for Pugin to explore the relationship between his architectural principles and his utopian social ideals, because they were complete communities from the start. As at Jesus College, the effect of architectural change on the community could be easily gauged and evaluated.

The return of Catholic education to England was a cause of great excitement to Pugin. As he had made plain in *Contrasts*, he believed Catholic institutions would play an essential part in transforming society more broadly.[2] Educational institutions provided another way of spreading the Catholic mission (in addition to books and architectural examples) and sent living people into the world to actively do God's work. Catholic churches required priests, and the new seminaries at Oscott, Ushaw, and Maynooth produced them. Pugin built at all three. Oscott, particularly, was the rock on which Pugin stood, his position as Professor of Ecclesiastical Antiquities giving him both authority and a platform for propagating his ideas.

Pugin claimed that institutional settings shape character: if an institution's buildings were Gothic, 'the mind [would be] most forcibly carried back to the days of England's faith'.[3] He was absolutely right that educational communities create identities. Shared space equals shared rituals and shared experience. The buildings of an organisation do not merely symbolise its structure, but actually embody it.[4] This idea fell under Pugin's concept of 'propriety', which he defined with the statement that 'the external and internal appearance of an edifice should be illustrative of, and in accordance with, the purpose for which it is destined'.[5]

Pugin believed that a learning environment should be beautiful, demonstrating the glories of Christian art. His hope was that, having seen the potential of such art, its graduates and faculty could spread pointed architecture as they went forth to commission new churches, new institutions, and new houses. He implored the seminarians he taught at Oscott not to 'consider the restoration of ancient art as a mere matter of taste, but remember that it is most closely connected with the revival of the faith itself'.[6] He even established a museum of medieval art at Oscott to provide them with inspiring examples. Catholic educational institutions, he hoped, could be hubs of a Gothic network. Unlike monasteries, with their relatively static population, educational institutions were constantly graduating students. The dark, stark quadrangle at Maynooth, to name just one example, sowed the seeds of the Gothic Revival in Ireland and resulted in a nation whose 19th-century Catholics were deeply devoted to the Puginian ideal.[7]

The quietly radical notion that environment played a role in education, with its implication that Gothic, especially, gave the greatest encouragement

The entrance to St Patrick's College, Maynooth. [Richard Butler]

to Christian character, would become a dominant idea in the design of universities in the English-speaking world. It generated countless ivy-covered Gothic quadrangles over the next hundred years, from Glasgow to Melbourne to Princeton.

The medieval example

Pugin's ideal Christian educational foundation was based on the medieval colleges of the University of Oxford. He considered Oxford's Magdalen College to be such a superlative example of a medieval educational complex that he devoted a full-page plate in *True Principles* to a reconstruction of its 15th-century appearance.

It was the only real medieval building to be illustrated in the book; the rest were Pugin's own 'ideal schemes'.

In order to understand Pugin's intentions, Magdalen's plan and organisation must be examined. The medieval Oxbridge college had evolved over the centuries in a consistent quadrangular form. The mature type first emerged during the second half of the 14th century, in two works of Bishop William of Wykeham, Winchester College and New College, Oxford. Magdalen College represented a particularly grand manifestation of the Wykehamite model. Chapel and hall, respectively the centres of religious

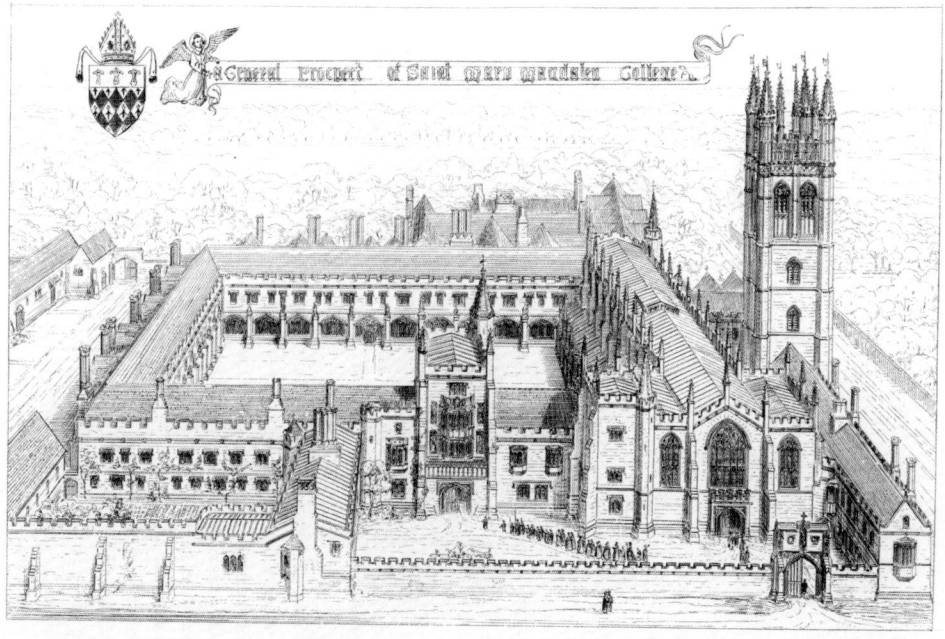

Magdalen College, Oxford, as portrayed in *True Principles*. [Public Domain]

and secular communal life, dominated one range of the quadrangle. As the largest spaces, these buildings were built back to back so that they could share a common structure. The chapel was the most elaborately ornamented part of the college, marking it as the central rationale of the college's existence as an organisation dedicated to the glory of God. Pugin felt that preferably the chapel should be emphasised by a tower.[8] English collegiate chapels were T-shaped with an antechapel forming the top of the T. The stem of the T was a chancel divided from the antechapel by a screen. This arrangement seems to have evolved accidentally, when the early 13th-century builders of Merton College, Oxford's chapel decided the cruciform church they had planned was too large for their needs and omitted the nave. The T-shape, however, proved to work well. Since the local community would be served by parish churches elsewhere in the town, no nave was necessary to seat them; the entire collegiate community could be seated in the chancel. As in monastic institutions, seating in the chancel consisted of inward-facing stalls, creating two sides ideal for antiphonal singing. Since the members of the college faced each other, it also served to reinforce the communal nature of worship. When not in use for worship, the chancel could be closed off with gates, with the antechapel serving the needs of private contemplation, or even being used for teaching divinity. The antechapel also provided a space where members of the community could be buried. Pugin adopted this T shape in all his collegiate designs, although the only one he was actually able to build was at Ushaw.

In the medieval Oxbridge model, the college quadrangle itself was a square paradise garden, its shape meant to imply the perfection and balance of God's creation. The collegiate community thus became a microcosm of the world. Over the entrance to the quadrangle was a gate tower, which often contained the master's lodgings, so that he could observe comings and goings. The other sides of the quadrangle contained housing for scholars and fellows, who were each given a suite of bedroom and study. The study was marked by a larger window than the bedroom, reflecting the use of the rooms, as more light would be needed for reading and writing. A library was located on the first floor of one of the ranges – raised above ground level to protect the books from vermin and damp. There would also be a muniment room to hold the charters that formed the legal basis of the college's existence as well as its other treasures, usually located in a tower and vaulted with stone to make it fireproof. As a group, for those who knew how to read them, these buildings expressed the ideal Christian community, clearly signalling their purpose both via design and via symbolic ornament, in the same way that Gothic churches did. For Pugin it was the ideal format, constantly reminding residents of their Christian purpose while providing the most efficient facilities for its enactment.

The paganising of learning

Pugin was deeply concerned that modern universities had moved away from this medieval format. He was troubled both by the use of Classical styles and by the secularisation of education, which, typically, he felt went hand in hand. The new London University was his bugbear,[9] for it was not a cloistered community, but a block of classrooms and offices by William Wilkins. Like Wilkins's National Gallery, the building was dominated by a central dome and portico that simply marked an atrium. Avowedly secular, in keeping with Jeremy Bentham's vision, it had no chapel. The universities of the Continent too, Pugin claimed, were being rebuilt as vast stucco-fronted blocks with no features to distinguish them from a barracks or an asylum. He wrote, 'How is it possible to expect that the race of men who proceed from these factories of learning will possess the same feelings as

St David's College, Lampeter, designed by C R Cockerell. [Public Domain]

those who anciently went forth from the Catholic structures of Oxford and Winchester!'[10]

The 'factories of learning', he feared, were stripping the civic and spiritual character out of education. A student of one of these colleges might gain a skill, but not the fully rounded character needed to best contribute to society. There was no rejoicing in shared community; the teacher-student relationship became transactional. Thus the university became another instrument of the dead, hollow commercialism that the church militant proposed to fight.

Pugin particularly blamed fellow architect Charles Robert Cockerell for building major Greek Revival edifices at both Oxford and Cambridge: 'A man who paganises in the Universities deserves no quarter'.[11] He felt that Cockerell was using his considerable talent and his position as Professor of Architecture at the Royal Academy to 'poison the minds of the students' against Gothic design.[12] It is true that Cockerell rarely designed in Gothic, and when he did, by Pugin's standards it was sterile. His design for the new college of St David's, Lampeter in south-west Wales, for instance, was symmetrical and flat with rows of identical windows borrowed from Georgian fenestration, the spatial hierarchy was weak, and the different functions of college spaces were unexpressed.

It was essentially a decorated box, its Gothic clothes meant to signal 'college'.

After the death of architect and educator John Soane, Cockerell had become the leading classicist in England, espousing rich, sculptural Greek designs (St David's College was an exception), which, like Pugin, he based on careful archaeological study yet modernised for Victorian needs. Cockerell had also taken the lead at Oxbridge. He was given the most prominent commissions to be awarded during Pugin's lifetime at both universities: the Cambridge University Library and Oxford's Ashmolean Museum.

The battle for Oxford

Pugin loved Oxford. It was one of the most complete medieval cities in England, crowned by its famous cluster of towers and spires. It was also the greatest scholastic centre to survive from the Middle Ages. It was a city where Pugin longed to work. If his theories were correct about the way Gothic architecture influenced those who experienced it, then Oxford's wealth of medieval architecture should have resulted in a strong 'Gothic spirit' in the university. And when Pugin first encountered Oxford that seemed to be the case. The city was the seat of the Tractarian Movement, whose leaders, such as John Henry Newman, Edward Bouverie Pusey, and John Keble, sought to bring certain Catholic doctrines that had been lost in the years since the Reformation back into the Church of England. They especially promoted ritual and sensory experience. Pugin had been one of the early voices in the debate over the propriety of ritual, concern over which formed a central issue of the Tractarian argument. The debate over ritual seemed to embroil the entire Anglican and Roman Catholic Churches in the 1840s. However, as a Catholic, Pugin had not experienced quite the same bitterness of controversy, because Roman Catholics already accepted the desirability of ritual as a baseline. For their part, the Tractarians shared Pugin's belief that a church building could be read symbolically and that churches should stir the emotions of worshippers. In practice, this often manifested itself in medievalism, as in Newman's church at Littlemore.[13]

In the 1840s, it was unclear where the Tractarian Movement was leading. Would the Church of England absorb these changes and retain the essential characteristics of Protestantism? Would the movement be stamped out as heretical, causing no permanent change at all? Or would the swelling popular movement lead many English Christians down the path to Rome, as many conservative Anglicans feared and Pugin dearly hoped? Already there had been a few conversions. Oxford was at the intellectual heart of the Church of England; it also trained the nation's future political and business leaders. If the trickle of conversions at Oxford became a stream, then perhaps the dream of re-Catholicising England could be accomplished with miraculous quickness, with whole Oxford colleges coming over and the nation following.

Low Church Protestants and traditional Anglicans were severely alarmed and fought to maintain the status quo. Oxford became a battleground. Theological arguments tore through the university. Some theologians were even defrocked and stripped of their fellowships.

Although architecture was to be a key weapon in the Tractarian cause, the Anti-Tractarians soon joined in the architectural fight as well. In 1838 they commissioned a tall stone monument, the Martyrs Memorial, in the prominent intersection of two major roads by which people approached the town.

It made a definitively Protestant statement at the entrance to central Oxford. The memorial was dedicated to three Protestant martyrs who had laid the doctrinal foundations of the Church of England. They had been subsequently tried and executed in Oxford during the brief re-establishment of Catholicism during the reign of Queen Mary. The inscription on the base of the new memorial proclaimed that these martyrs had affirmed sacred truths 'against the errors of the Church of Rome'.

The Martyrs Memorial was designed by the young George Gilbert Scott, newly aflame with Gothic zeal kindled by the writings of Pugin. Its form was inspired by 13th-century Eleanor crosses, which Edward I had built as memorials to his queen, a model suitable to Pugin's principles. Yet, ideologically, what the memorial represented could not have been further from

Martyrs' Memorial, Oxford; the Ashmolean can be seen behind. [Henry Taunt/Historic England Archive CC51/00647]

Pugin's beliefs. Pugin was infuriated by it. He wrote a pamphlet attacking it and shocked Oxford's sense of propriety by delivering it to the heads of colleges in person.[14]

The new cross stood opposite the rising Ashmolean. A Grecian style made sense for a building intended to house Classical sculpture and Renaissance paintings, one which introduced the latest ideas in museum design borrowed from the neo-Classical sculpture galleries of Munich and Berlin. Yet Cockerell's university art gallery was seen as an outrage by devotees of the Gothic Revival. Pugin called it a 'gin-palace', and Ruskin refused to lecture in it.[15]

However, unexpectedly in 1843, Pugin's luck at Oxford seemed to change. He was invited to submit designs for the rebuilding of Balliol College – the greatest opportunity of his career to design a prominent educational institution – and on a site adjacent to the Martyrs' Memorial no less! Balliol was a medieval foundation that had all but lost its medieval fabric. A literal revival of its medieval glories, with the concomitant restructuring of institutional life around Sarum Rite worship and communal meals in an oak-beamed great hall, could not have been more to Pugin's liking.

Starting in the 1850s, Oxford would face an avalanche of Gothic Revival construction with the building of Deane and Woodward's University Museum, with George Edmund Street designing Gothic churches and school houses for the new suburbs of Puginian villas, with Ruskin lecturing as Slade Professor, and with the High Victorian, High Church Keble College rising in its spiky polychromatic glory near the University Parks. However, in 1843, the eventual victory of Pugin's principles was by no means given. 1843 was

Oxford Shire Hall, designed by John Plowman Jr. [Author]

the same year that Edward Blore completed a dreary Gothicising of St John's College Chapel, sweeping away a screen by Christopher Wren only to replace it with the sort of flat, applied ornament and repetitive detailing that Pugin abhorred. Oxford's Shire Hall by John Plowman Jr, completed only two years previously, was the sort of castellated Georgian that Pugin felt was literally and figuratively completely indefensible.[16]

Oxford had long felt the need to reference the medieval past in its architecture, but the way it had done so, with the sole exception of the Martyrs Memorial, was by applying decorative Gothic trappings. The Balliol project gave Pugin the chance to introduce his true principles to Oxford.

Civil war in Balliol

When Pugin arrived on the scene, Balliol's Broad Street front was approaching a state of near dilapidation.

Its repair and expansion was a pressing need. The fellows had approached their usual architect, George Basevi, but the drawings he produced in a competent but unexciting and old-fashioned version of the Gothic Revival style were rejected by the fellows. At that point, two fellows with Tractarian sympathies, W G Ward and Frederick Oakley, requested permission to write to Pugin. They hoped that Balliol could be convinced to build something at the cutting edge of the Gothic Revival. Permission was granted, but the master, Richard Jenkyns, added the caveat that if Pugin's design were approved by the college's Governing Body, they would have to be carried out by another architect. He did not want the college to be perceived as supporting such a controversial Catholic figure.[17]

Realising that the request from Balliol was not a commission but merely a proposal, Pugin aimed to impress them enough that they could not fail to award him the project. The Balliol proposal gave him an opportunity to design the ideal college that he had not been able to fully explore in *True Principles*. He worked it out to a minute level of detail, producing dozens of drawings for everything from the staircase in the master's lodging to the garden gate.

When he was done, he sent a set of plans and elevations to the Governing Body but he also had a volume of evocative perspective sketches bound with velvet and brass. He sent this to the fellows who had approached him.

At the front of the volume was an illuminated dedication page showing the college founders kneeling reverently on either side of his new design. A birds-eye view in the manner of David Loggan, with illuminated coats of arms in the corners, showed his proposal in its entirety. The Broad Street front was to be rebuilt with a classic Oxford embattled muniments tower bearing niches with statues of the founders and patron saint. The walls were to be of local Headington ashlar in keeping with Oxford tradition

The Broad Street façade of Balliol College, Oxford, roughly as Pugin would have known it. [Historic England Archive CC50/00895]

(although Pugin recognised that this stone degrades quickly and specified Caen stone for the dressings). The fenestration was irregular, with oriels marking important rooms. In keeping with his specifications for collegiate architecture in *True Principles*, projecting chimneys acted as buttresses. The master's lodging was to be entirely rebuilt, becoming a small manor house with its own smaller entrance tower fused onto the side of the Broad Street frontage. Although some other colleges had moved their masters off site in order to make space for more classrooms and offices, Pugin said that a true community of scholars must have a master living on site. The hall was to have a new traceried louvre in the centre of a hammer-beam roof, and there would be a new stone kitchen with an octagonal roof, a showpiece fusing the design of the two great surviving medieval kitchens at Glastonbury and

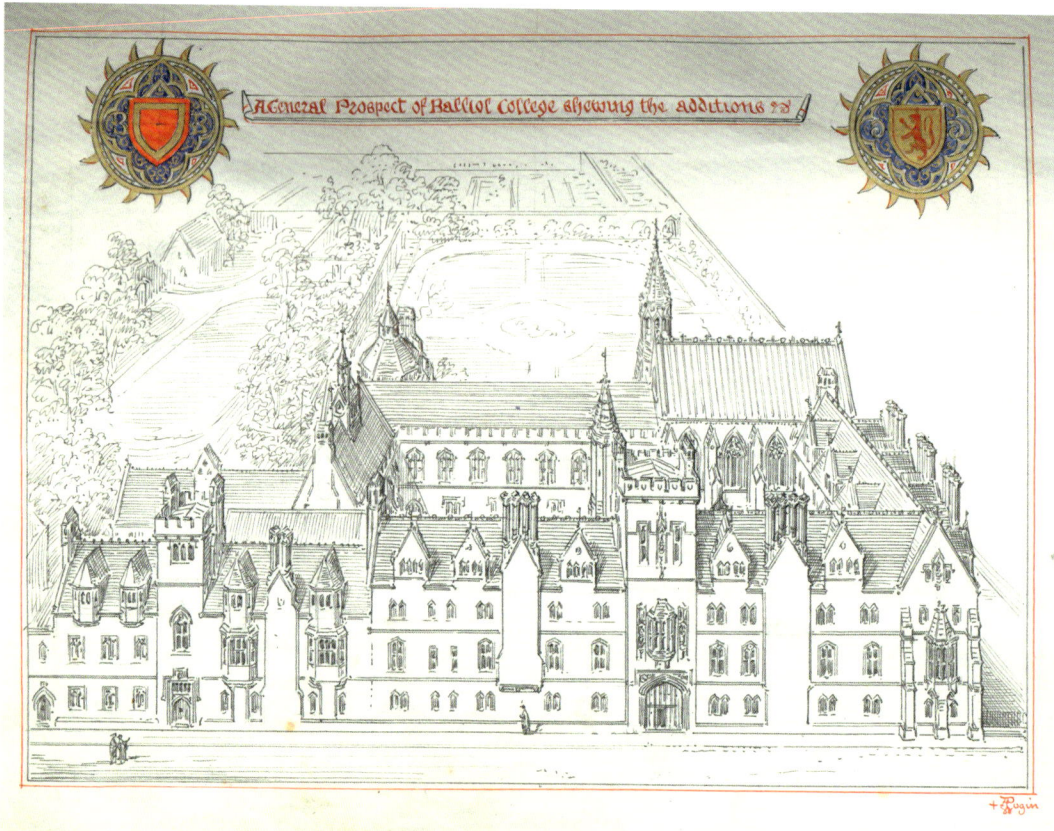

A General Prospect of Balliol College shewing the additions &c

Birds-eye view of Pugin's proposed renovation of Balliol College. [The Master and Fellows of Balliol College, Oxford]

Stanton Harcourt. The kitchen would stand independently in the Fellows' Garden like the chapter house of a cathedral. Finally, the 16th-century chapel would be demolished to make way for a new one with a belfry turret, inward-facing stalls, and an elaborately decorated sanctuary. Remarkably, Pugin went so far as to specify the medieval Catholic lifestyles of the buildings' occupants. Students' and fellows' rooms were portrayed with structural Gothic furniture, prie dieux set up before devotional paintings, Latin mottoes on the walls, and many portraits of bishops.

The arrival of Pugin's designs at Balliol prompted a controversy so violent, that it was nicknamed 'The Civil War of 1843'.[18] Conservative Anglicans stood their ground against the Tractarian fellows who supported Pugin, and neither side was willing to back down. The discussion of the plans by the Governing Body was so disputatious that the pages recording the meeting

Proposed Balliol College kitchen. [The Master and Fellows of Balliol College, Oxford]

Proposed staircase in the Master's Lodgings. [The Master and Fellows of Balliol College, Oxford]

were later ordered to be removed from the minutes book and destroyed. The master, however, put an end to the matter. Calling the fellows together in the chapel, he declared, in so many words, that the statutes of the college committed it to the defence of Protestantism and that he was using his authority to prohibit the enactment of Pugin's plans. That put an end to the controversy, and, just to be safe, the master successfully barred all new construction until his death a decade later. Balliol then invited the architect William Butterfield to build a new chapel in memory of the late master, based largely on Pugin's designs.[19] The new chapel was pure Puginian Gothic and outfitted for High Anglican worship, complete with a chancel screen.

Pugin was bitterly disappointed with the outcome at Balliol. As much as he loved Oxford, he would remain too controversial a figure to ever be employed on a substantial project there. In 1844 his scheme for rebuilding Magdalen College School would also be rejected. His close friend J R Bloxam, however, did manage to arrange for him to design a new High Street gate and some wallpaper for Magdalen College. The Magdalen gate would be Pugin's only built Oxford work.

Pugin was particularly pleased to be permitted to demolish a 1635 gate believed to have been designed by Inigo Jones, the architect who had first brought Renaissance Classicism to Britain. By doing so he made the front quadrangle fully Gothic once again. In keeping with the true principle of honest construction that expressed its purpose, Pugin wrote that he had 'treated it as a mere arch in a wall'.[20] Even a gate by Pugin was so

Gateway to Magdalen College, Oxford. [Henry Taunt/Historic England Archive HT00721]

controversial that the plan had to be kept secret. It was prefabricated in the workshop of George Myers so that it could be trucked in and erected as quickly as possible – a *fait accompli* before a controversy had time to develop. When it was noticed that Magdalen had a new gateway by Pugin, it elicited a storm of comment in the press.

Cambridge

In utter contrast to his experience at Oxford, when Pugin was invited to design a building for the University of Cambridge, it went remarkably smoothly. There seems to have been no parallel to the uproar at Balliol. His work on the chapel of Jesus College, Cambridge, was his most prestigious Anglican commission. It was also his most important work of restoration of an existing medieval fabric. The job went well because the circumstances of the commission were somewhat different.

Pugin was invited to renovate the chapel at the urging of the aforementioned organist, John Sutton, a wealthy landowner and college fellow. Sutton had probably first met Pugin in 1845, when his father, Richard Sutton, had commissioned him to design a family tomb in the parish church of West Tofts, Norfolk. The following year, the 26-year-old John Sutton had married, but his wife had fallen ill and died within one month of the wedding. The widowed Sutton was subsequently elected a Fellow-Commoner of Jesus College, although his formal education consisted only of two years at Eton. By the end of 1846, he had moved into college rooms, and devoted himself to studying the history of music. He would work with Pugin to design an organ for West Tofts, and the two would write a small book on organ design together in 1847. Sutton also commissioned Pugin to design an organ and some chancel furnishings for Jesus College Chapel, which he would donate in memory of his wife.

When Pugin visited the chapel to take measurements for the organ, he offered advice about how to repair the tower, which had been structurally weakened by earlier restoration works carried out by the architect Anthony Salvin.[21] Sutton then offered to fund a complete restoration of the chapel, if the college would commission Pugin as its architect.

The Jesus College work allowed a rare glimpse of Pugin as a restorer. Pugin lived in a time when medieval buildings were sorely treated; even the colleges of Oxford and Cambridge had hidden medieval ceilings behind pastel-coloured plaster vaults and replaced leaded medieval glass with large modern panes. When he arrived at Jesus College, Pugin set about taking it back to a medieval appearance. In addition to the already mentioned furnishings and the repair of the tower, he took down and rebuilt the entire east wall of the chancel. During this work, he removed a 15th-century Perpendicular east window that had been installed when the buildings were

Sketch of an angel
seemingly intended
to decorate an organ
designed by Pugin and
Sutton. [Yale Center
for British Art, Paul
Mellon Collection
B1977.14.20608]

Interior of Jesus College Chapel, showing the lancets installed by Pugin at the east end. [Author]

converted into a college in the 15th century. He replaced it with three tall lancets.[22]

The new lancets were closely related to the impressive 13th-century arcade on the north wall, thus giving unity to the space. He justified the replacement of a genuine medieval window with new work by claiming that he was taking the chapel back to its original 13th-century appearance. To support this, he cited the discovery of fragments of medieval lancets in the dismantled chancel wall. Pugin's philosophy of restoration was parallel to that of George Gilbert Scott, who on many more occasions than Pugin proved willing to remove genuine late medieval work in order to reconstruct a building's original appearance based on fragmentary archaeological evidence. Pugin also removed the low-pitched 15th-century chancel roof to replace it with a higher-pitched one that he believed more closely approximated the 13th-century original.

The restoration of the Jesus Chapel cost approximately £5,000, a sum that exceeded the budget of many of Pugin's new churches. Sutton, however, was wealthy, and the figure was less than a tithing percentage of his annual income. The master of Jesus College, William French, did not like to see the college being led along by a rich donor and hinted that there may have been some ideological reservations about aspects of Pugin's work – but Sutton had the support of many of the fellows and the chapel structure needed to be stabilised, so the work was quietly allowed to go ahead. The renovation was completed in 1849. The following year the master died, and was replaced by the Evangelical, G E Corrie. Although Corrie objected to the changes that had been made in the chapel, he found that now that the modifications were complete and the new boys' choir was endowed, there was little he could do to change the way worship was conducted. It was exactly the sort of outcome Pugin would have wanted. The new ritualistic worship was literally set in stone.

The monastic orders return

With Catholic Emancipation the monastic orders returned to the United Kingdom and established bases for their work. For the first time in hundreds of years, the black and white habits of the Trappists were seen in Leicestershire's Charnwood Forest. Nuns built convents from which they could care for the poor of industrial cities where nuns had never before dwelt. Naturally, as Catholic patrons began to commission buildings for these religious communities, many of them turned to Pugin. Ten convents and one (or perhaps two) monasteries were built to his designs.[23] With the exception of the priory that he built for the Trappists at Mount St Bernard, Leicestershire, Pugin's monastic buildings were all designed for modern, non-cloistered orders.

Design for St Bernard's Abbey, as illustrated in *Present State*. [Public Domain]

The majority of Pugin's convents were built for the Religious Sisters of Mercy, founded in Ireland in 1831; he also built for the Presentation Brothers and Sisters (another modern Irish order) and the Loreto Sisters. These orders engaged in the active provision of Catholic social services that Pugin championed in his writings. They were devoted to ministering to society at large, caring for the poor, the sick and the needy. In addition to the usual residential facilities, they required schoolrooms for teaching local children. The novel nature of these orders meant that Pugin essentially had to invent a building type from scratch, as there were no direct medieval precedents.

As he had with his house designs, Pugin turned to the rambling masonry buildings in 17th-century prints by Hollar, Merian, and Loggan.[24]

These images showed English domestic and commercial architecture before the age of industrialisation, buildings suitable for adaptation to what were essentially large residences. Pugin distinguished his work from other

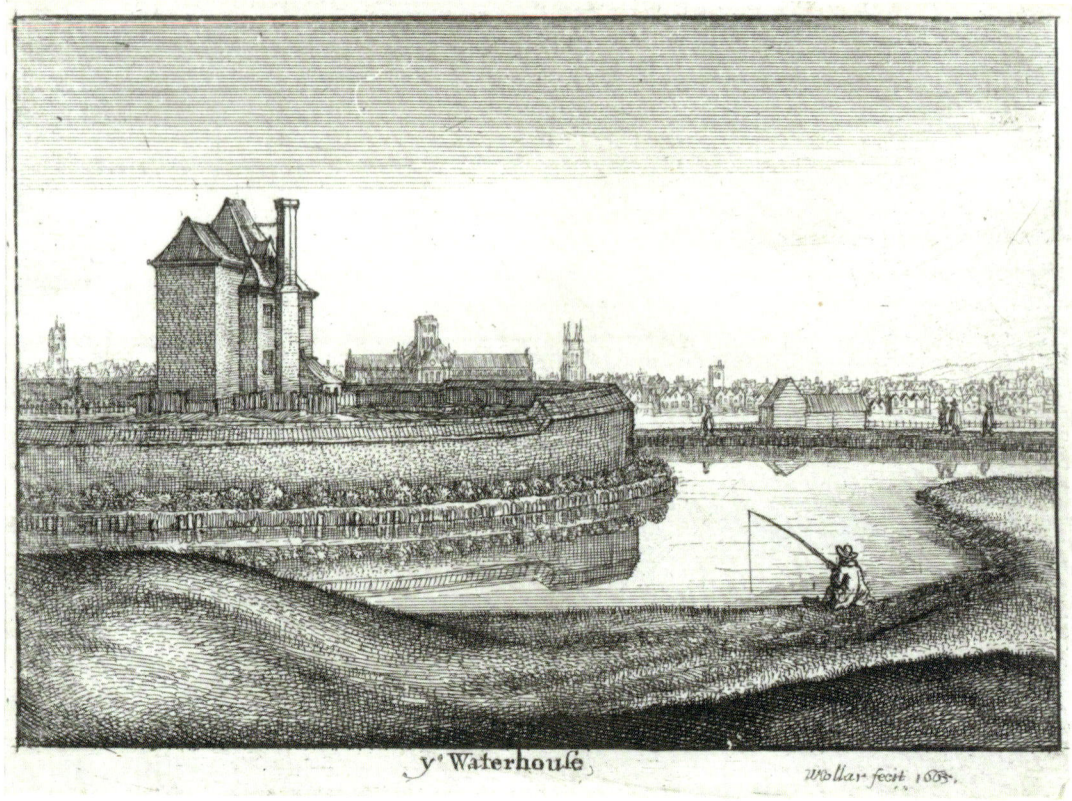

y' Waterhouse

Etching of the Waterhouse by Wenceslaus Hollar. [Public Domain]

recently designed monasteries and convents by looking to these vernacular precedents. Georgian primness was banished; the massing was rough – all chimneys and roof slopes – 'natural', as Pugin liked to say, in its response to functional needs. From the prints, Pugin learned to group masses with some wings projecting or receding barely a few feet, braced as needed with chimneys and buttresses, with no regard for symmetry. He did not cultivate the rusticity and irregular hand-crafted textures of the later Arts and Crafts Movement. Instead, buildings were translated into Victorian industrial materials – the soft, timeworn Tudor brick house was interpreted with sharp edges, strict levels, and hard, mechanical smoothness.

Larger institutional buildings provided greater opportunities for picturesque effects than residential villas did; there were more chimneys to group, more towers, more turrets and cresting, more buildings to arrange. The convent for the Presentation Sisters at Waterford was particularly lovely, a

Convent of the Presentation, Waterford. [Richard Butler]

stone quadrangle buttressed by chimneys with a round tower and conical
roof that gave it the air of a minor chateau.

Pugin placed these buildings with Romantic sensitivity to their position
in the landscape. The almshouses at Alton, home to a non-monastic
Catholic community, were set on the edge of a rise near the castle ruins,
with the rooms in the north range designed to take advantage of sweeping
views out over the valley. The south range looked out over sheltered
gardens. Winding paths to the castle were 'well suited to the meditation
of its aged inmates'.[25] At Mount St Bernard, the setting was 'exceedingly
wild and romantic', with 'irregular masses of granite rocks' and 'extensive
prospects' over the surrounding barren, rocky hills.[26] The farmland culti-
vated by the brothers contrasted sharply with the desolate surroundings,
and Pugin hoped to place a calvary on the summit of a nearby rock, thereby
sacralising the landscape.

Corridor of Ushaw College. [Author]

In these rambling monastic buildings, the developments of Pugin's house architecture met those of his church designs. Within the limited budgets of his convents, the matchstick trusses first developed for his church roofs reappeared to shelter libraries and refectories. Narrow boards were turned on edge to make rafters over corridors. The primary unit of planning was the quadrangle, which for smaller complexes, such as the almshouses at Alton, was broken open into a U-shaped plan. The quadrangle edges were lined with long corridors, enclosed cloisters that accommodated the Victorian desire for thermal comfort.

Pugin tapped these long corridors to create the primary spatial drama of these simple buildings. They had lean-to roofs open to the rafters, tiled floors, and pointed arch windows in thick, plastered walls. The accompanying refectories were usually simple, rectangular rooms, with tiled floors, and perhaps dado panelling, corbeled beams, or a carved fireplace. The chapel, of course, was the richest space, but often simple still, and in many cases it doubled as a schoolroom. At Alton, as in some of the convents, the nave could be closed off from the chancel by doors in the chancel arch, and the benches had fold-out desks. The simple interiors were as far as could be from the bold colour, patterns, and rich carving of Pugin's country house work. All was simplicity and restraint, whites and browns with a bit of black or yellow in the tiles; often the only decoration was a crucifix on a plain white wall. It was to such buildings that Pugin was referring when he talked of the simplicity and economy of the Gothic style.

Monastic clients

Pugin's first convent was built in Bermondsey in 1838. This was right at the beginning of his career, only a year after his first church in Reading. Pugin did not start out as a church-builder and diversify later as his reputation grew, but began with his full range, building churches, decorating country houses, designing villas and institutions all within the first three years of his practice. His first convent was apparently barely habitable. He often clashed with his monastic clients when they asked for large sash windows rather than mullioned lights in their cells, or when they objected to the perceived discomfort of his cold, tiled refectories, but the complaints about the Bermondsey convent exceeded the usual difference of opinion. When the head of the Religious Sisters of Mercy, Mother Catherine McAuley, went to inspect the new convent she wrote, 'the heart of the foundress sank as she walked through the bleak corridors ... the house, more like a tomb than a modern dwelling, was in the monastic style of some far-away century'.[27] She continued in another letter, 'I do not admire Mr Pugin's taste ... He was determined we should not look out of the windows – they are up in the ceiling'. And yet, when she had to work with Pugin again on a

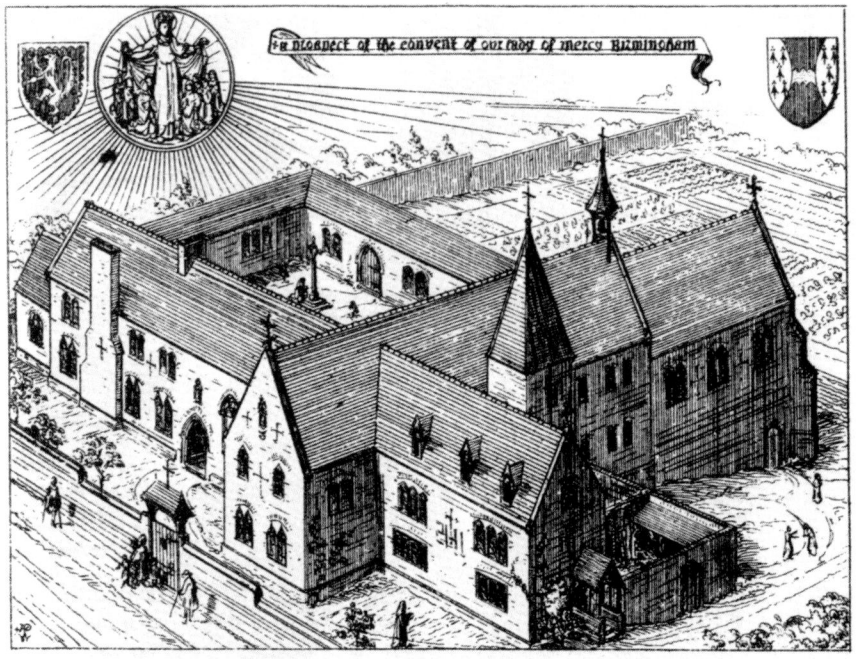

Convent of the Religious Sisters of Mercy, Birmingham, as illustrated in *Present State*. [Public Domain]

Convent of the Religious Sisters of Mercy, Birmingham, as built. [© Historic England Archive AA42/00188]

convent at Handsworth, Birmingham, two years later, she professed herself pleased.

In that case, the commission had come directly from Pugin's friend John Hardman for a convent next to his house, and the sisters had little say in the choice of architect. Built on a hillside, the enclosed Birmingham cloister stepped its way down a gentle slope.[28] The Sisters were so pleased that they went on to commission six more convents from Pugin.

Downside

In echo of Balliol, Pugin's greatest monastic commission went unbuilt. This was the design for Downside Abbey in Somerset, the senior community of the Benedictines in England.

Pugin presented an ideal scheme in a bird's-eye view with large quadrangles running off the edge of the sheet to imply that the project could be extended indefinitely as the community grew. A large cruciform

Unexecuted design for Downside Abbey. [Yale Center for British Art, Paul Mellon Collection B1977.14.20665]

church with three broach spires was somewhat like St Chad's, Birmingham, but larger. The nave was long and the east end a cluster of chapels, like the one he designed for the cathedral at Nottingham. The complex was to have contained a much broader range of facilities than his other, smaller monastic buildings: lecture rooms, an infirmary, guest rooms and a hall for feeding and sheltering visitors, a chapel for the sick. The main cloister was to have been 150 feet (45 meters) square. Pugin dreamed of an abbey the size of Glastonbury or Gloucester, but the English Benedictines had only recently returned to the United Kingdom and did not yet have the numbers or the finances for a return to the scale that they had achieved in the Middle Ages. The monks balked at the expense of the entire scheme, prevaricating for five years before finally cancelling the project.

Throughout his career, it was Pugin's grandest projects that failed. 'I have passed my life in thinking of fine things, studying fine things, designing fine things, and realizing very poor ones', he complained.[29] His Anglican clients at Balliol perhaps would have had the resources to construct one of his ideal schemes. The English Catholic Church, as demonstrated at Downside, but also at St George's Cathedral in Southwark, simply did not. The Irish Catholic Church also had limited resources, and although Parliament voted to grant a substantial sum to pay for Pugin's seminary buildings at Maynooth, the money was insufficient for the large buildings required. When faced with these commissions for some of the most important Catholic sites in England and Ireland, Pugin refused to compromise. His clients were sometimes sympathetic – they too wanted to see Catholicism reclaim its lost glory – but Pugin often frustrated them with his failure to be realistic.

The Hospital of St John the Baptist, Alton

Thus, it was with smaller-scale projects that Pugin was often able to erect his greatest works. Among his institutional works, one such smaller project, the almshouses known as the Hospital of St John the Baptist, Alton, were particularly dear to him, because dignified care for the poor was a significant part of his vision for the return of Catholicism.

It was begun in 1839, the year that Thomas Carlyle published his essay on 'the condition of England'.[30] Extreme economic inequality was a major political concern, and the nation was rocked by the Chartist threat of working-class insurrection. At Alton, Pugin and Lord Shrewsbury constructed a model almshouse, one that provided the elderly poor with housing and meals, spiritual care, country walks, reading, and a sense of community. It also provided schooling for poor local children. The almshouse was placed at the edge of the village, so as to remain an integral part of it. As a paternalistic gesture towards his tenants, Lord Shrewsbury

Aerial view of Alton Castle and the Hospital of St John the Baptist. [Donated by Bob Metcalf/ Staffordshire Past Track]

funded the project and provided ground on his estate, employing a warden, schoolmaster, and chaplains. Different generations and different social classes were thus brought together in harmonious society. The ideal scheme for an 'Antient Poor House' that Pugin would add to the 1843 edition of *Contrasts*, was largely the result of the ideas he had put into practice at Alton.

The engraving, which contrasted the almshouse with a modern workhouse, could not have put his and Lord Shrewsbury's aims more plainly. Even the picturesque architecture of St John's was in contrast to the cheap, dehumanising monotony of workhouse buildings.[31]

The hope was that such works of charity would grow from their humble beginnings to serve larger and larger segments of the community. Like country houses, institutions tended to be added to and modified over time, and Pugin designed with this in mind. At Mount St Bernard, for instance, his original priory has been extended by additions and a vast abbey church had been constructed. At Ushaw College, Pugin's chapel soon proved too small for the growing community, so it was demolished and replaced by a new one. The Pugin stained glass and fittings were preserved and installed in the new

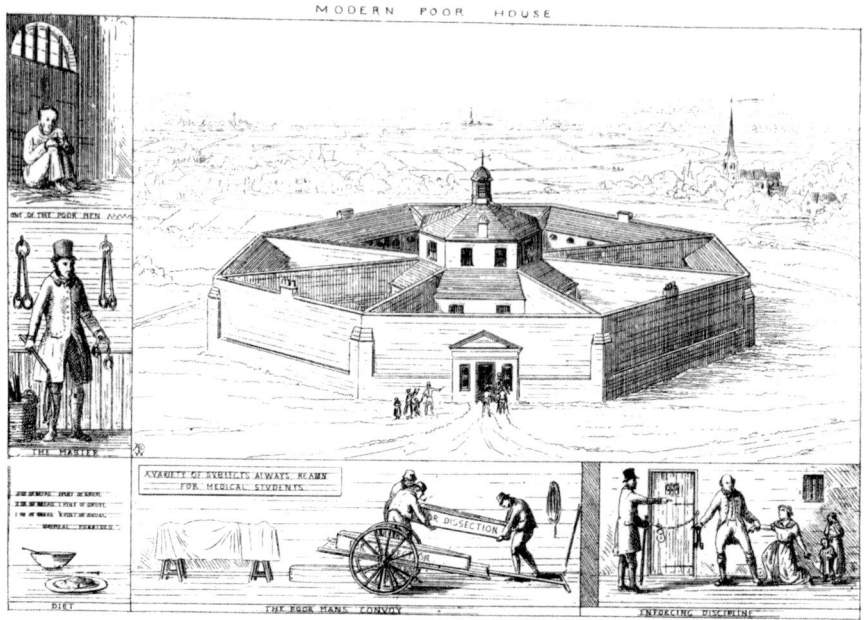

'Contrasted Residences for the Poor', as illustrated in the second edition of *Contrasts*.
[Public Domain]

building. Ushaw grew considerably over the next 100 years and continued to employ a member of the Pugin family as its architect. The whole complex pulses with Puginian spirit. The continued growth of Catholicism in Britain was something that Pugin fervently hoped for, and Ushaw was a good example of exactly the sort of growth he hoped his institutions would undergo. His entire architectural vision was organic: he expected churches, and houses too, to grow in elaboration as the years progressed, just as they had throughout British history.

4 The golden throne

In 1843 Pugin boldly prophesied that the new Houses of Parliament would be 'the morning star of the great revival of national architecture and art … if the architect's design for the great tower be carried out, we shall have a monument of English art which has not been surpassed even in antiquity'.[1] When the modern city was infused with Gothic spirit, he believed, it could develop into something superior to the city of the Middle Ages. The Houses of Parliament was the first sign of what that modernity might look like. Pugin was correct about the building's greatness. The new Palace of Westminster, especially its clocktower, metonymically known as 'Big Ben' after the bronze bell that booms out the hours, has undoubtedly become a symbol of Britain.

It is one of the world's most recognised buildings. Even its sound is familiar; the striking of its bells is broadcast daily by the BBC.

The French architect, Jean-Baptiste-Antione Lassus, whose restoration of the Ste Chapelle was admired by Pugin, declared of the Palace of Westminster in 1852, 'Seen … in fine moonlight, or under certain effects of clouds … it is a fairy palace, a marvel of the Thousand and One Nights'.[2] Claude Monet would paint the Houses of Parliament more than half a dozen times, and Kenneth Clark wrote that 'no painter can resist them'.[3] Hollywood directors also could not resist them: the building has appeared in countless films and television shows as cinematic shorthand for Britain. It appears in nearly every James Bond film and in science-fiction is the target of alien attacks. In Disney's *Peter Pan*, Peter and the Darling children paused during their flight across London to drift down onto the giant clock hand, with the clock face glowing like the moon behind them.

That clock hand and clock face were designed by A W N Pugin. This instantly recognisable clock is surely Pugin's best-known work. And yet there is an irony here, because Pugin's best-known work was not entirely his own design. The official architect of the Houses of Parliament was Charles Barry. The clock was Pugin's creation, but the cupola and roofline were Barry's. The tower's profile, like that of a giant grandfather clock, showed the hand of both architects.[4] This was the way it was throughout the entire

The clocktower of the Houses of Parliament. [© Historic England Archive AA077050]

building: the plan, the structure, and some of the decoration were Barry's; many of the details and some of the big ideas, were Pugin's. The palace that resulted from this collaboration was truly the best that the early Victorian world had to offer – a building with the measure and balance of Classicism and the rational planning of the academy, combined with the structural clarity and narrative ornament of the Gothic Revival. Numerous scientific experts assisted the architects so that the palace also incorporated the latest advances in ventilation, geology and lighting. It was important in a time of political upheaval that Parliament seem rational and scientifically grounded.[5]

Work on the building filled a large part of Pugin's career. He first assisted Barry with his competition designs in 1836, drafting Barry's entry at St Marie's Grange. In 1852, he drew the Big Ben clock face at the desk in his library at Ramsgate, only months before his final illness. The scale of the new palace was enormous, so it is no wonder that Pugin spent almost his entire career working on it. With legislative chambers, offices, libraries, restaurants, grand processional routes to accommodate public ritual, even an official residence for the Speaker, the palace's 262-metre façade along the Thames is still the longest façade in central London.[6] The building was so large that its structure would be far from completed when Barry died in 1860. Its decoration would continue well into the 20th century.

The old Palace of Westminster had been the traditional seat of Parliament since the Middle Ages. Although technically a royal palace, by the time of the Reformation the monarch seldom used it, and over the years Parliament had much modified the buildings to suit its own needs. When Pugin was a teenager, John Soane had made the latest in that series of modifications, adding a curved Gothic carriage entrance and a series of committee rooms for the House of Lords. In 1834, however, the palace was ravaged by fire. The most important medieval space was saved – Westminster Hall with its marvellously engineered timber roof – but the rest of the palace was all but destroyed. The young Pugin had watched it burn, pleased to see the faux-medieval 'cement pinnacles and battlements flying and cracking'.[7] He realised that the destruction would clear the way for one of the greatest architectural projects of his lifetime, a chance to demonstrate the highest capabilities of British art and architecture. After a series of false starts, Parliament called a national competition for the rebuilding, specifying that designs should be Gothic or Elizabethan in style. Pugin, who was just beginning his practice as an architect, was too inexperienced to contemplate making his own entry. However, two of the competitors, Gillespie Graham and Charles Barry, hired him to help with their own submissions.

It was Gothic detailing for which Pugin first became known. Because of his wide reading and careful study of medieval buildings and artefacts, he

King Edward's School, Birmingham, designed by Charles Barry. [Courtesy of the King Edward's Foundation Archive]

could design more convincing Gothic detail than anyone else of his generation. The architect Gillespie Graham had first hired him in 1835 to design details for the chapel of George Heriot's School, Edinburgh. Later in the same year, Charles Barry had commissioned him to design ornament for the King Edward VI Grammar School in Birmingham.

Trained as classicists, architects such as Barry and Graham were out of their depths when Gothic suddenly became fashionable. They treated Gothic as merely a cladding applied as an associational or historical statement rather than, as Pugin regarded it, an entire functional system. Pugin was brought in to design pinnacles, ceilings, fixtures, panelling and furniture – in these cases he was essentially a decorator, though he did not hesitate to suggest modifications to the main design. Both Graham and Barry were evidently pleased with his work and convinced of his abilities, because it was at the end of that year they had each hired him to help with their designs for the Parliament competition.[8]

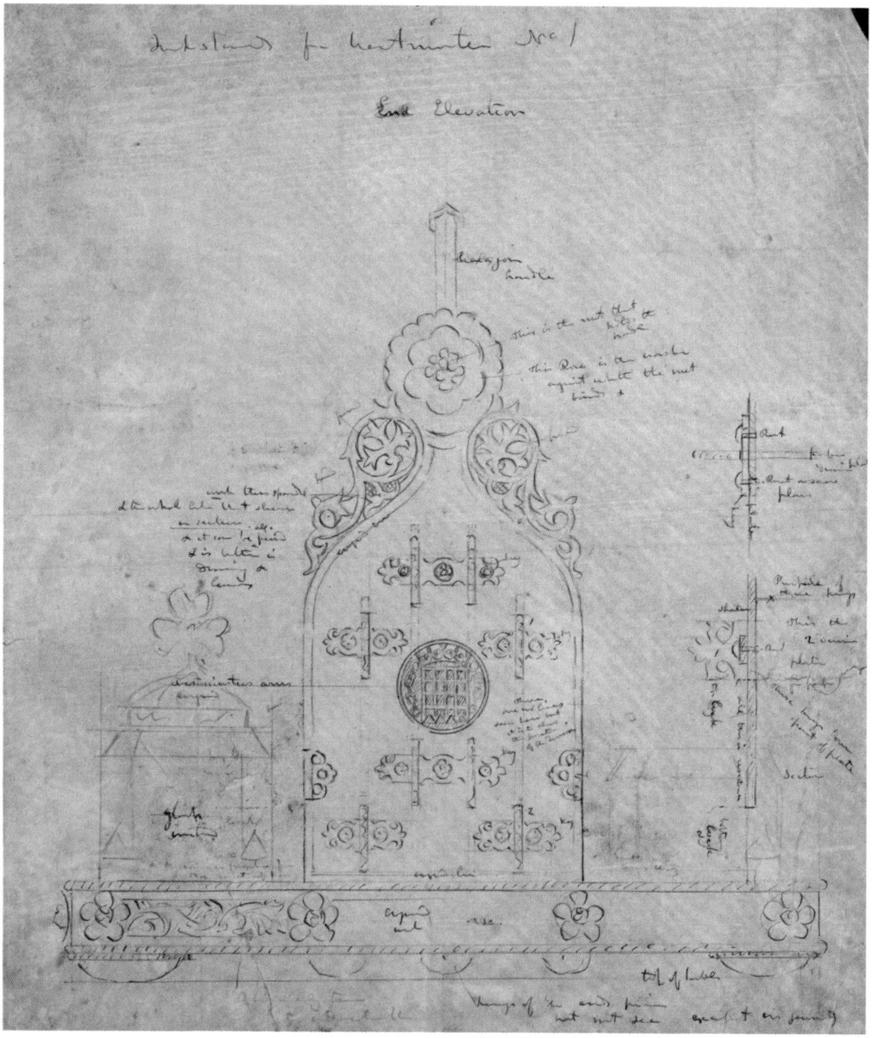

Barry won, and Pugin helped him to prepare estimate drawings, which were finished at the beginning of 1837. Then Barry began the construction drawings alone. By 1844, however, he recognised that he needed Pugin's help and had the humility to invite him back onboard. The House of Lords chamber was behind schedule, and Barry could not get the detailing right. He wanted the very best for the nation, and he knew that Pugin was the only designer in Britain who could breathe life into the detailing. Right away, Pugin began producing drawings for the project at a prodigious rate of speed, filling the chamber with rambling brass roses, rampant lions, stern ancient kings, and gilt armorials. Then, moving on to the rest of the building, he designed braced-timber tables, desk calendars and notice boards, chairs embossed with the portcullis logo, bookcases, floriated doorknobs, umbrella stands, and inkwells.

The nature of the collaboration

Pugin's involvement with the design was a widely known secret. His official title was Superintendent of Wood-Carving, a relatively minor post with meagre pay, which meant that the magnitude of his role went unacknowledged. However, it also meant that he did not have to deal with committees. Instead, he could report directly to Barry and get on with his work. He seemed happy with this arrangement, which was in keeping with the terms he had set out for Barry near the beginning of their collaboration.[9] Appointing Pugin to a minor position allowed him to be officially involved, thus giving him access to the site, but kept controversy from arising over his Catholicism or his being hired to make decorative designs without a competition.

After Barry and Pugin died, their sons would feud publicly about who the 'real' designer of the Houses of Parliament was, publishing a series of muck-raking pamphlets. The truth, of course, was that it was a collaboration. Barry was a tolerably good designer in Perpendicular Gothic, and the building's bones were all his – the long rows of Perpendicular windows admitting light from interior courtyards, the designs for the vaulting, the repeating blind tracery panels.[10] The modularity of the structure and decor created a measured rhythm. If Barry had designed the palace alone, he would still have created a stately abode for Parliament. Perhaps it would have been a little dry. Pugin's details allowed the building to be at once jovial and dignified.

Charles Barry's competition design for the Houses of Parliament, as revised after he won the competition in 1836. [RIBA Collections RIBA53363]

Design for an inkstand for the Palace of Westminster. [Yale Center for British Art, Paul Mellon Collection B1977.14.20590]

If Pugin had designed the palace alone (never a real possibility because of his Catholicism and his youth at the time of the competition), the building would have undoubtedly been a riotous picturesque Camelot, with heavy buttressed walls strewn with turrets and gilded finials.[11] However, Pugin lacked Barry's experience with large complex plans; Pugin's palace would have likely lacked the unity and rationality of Barry's building. And Pugin was always terrible with committees.

No, it was undoubtedly the combination of the two that gave the palace its magic. On the details that mattered most, Barry and Pugin collaborated closely. They sometimes met for days at a time, discussing ideas and sketching. Then Pugin would go back to The Grange to produce the necessary drawings. When the drawings arrived, Barry did not simply apply Pugin's designs. He worked over the important details carefully, modifying them to fit his ideas. Pugin was impressed by Barry and pleased to be working for him.[12] It seems that their relationship was always cordial, though strained towards the end because of Barry's failure to pay Pugin what he was owed.

The throne in the House of Lords' chamber and its canopy were a particular point of collaboration.

As the symbolic and aesthetic heart of the chamber, Barry knew this feature had to be just right, and he had consulted Pugin about it even during the years when Pugin was not officially involved in the project – a Pugin sketch of ideas for the canopy survives from 1841. Pugin ultimately

The throne in the House of Lords. [Public Domain]

designed the throne itself, which he derived from the Coronation Chair in Westminster Abbey.[13] Meanwhile, Barry worked to tone down Pugin's effervescent canopy, which initially featured an ogee arch and gable, simplifying Pugin's design into a more restrained rectangular arrangement. This made the throne a strong, but less dominant presence on the 364 days a year when the monarch was not present.

Art and ceremony

On the occasion that the monarch was present, however, at the annual state opening of Parliament, the involvement of Pugin, master of ritual, shone as brightly as the gilding. The glittering chamber of the House of Lords was the part of the palace on which Pugin had the greatest effect.

Many other spaces in the ceremonial route were decorated later, and Pugin and Barry's House of Commons, which was never critically acclaimed

The chamber of the House of Lords. [Historic England Archive CC97_01389]

and had acoustical problems, would be destroyed during the Second World War. But the climax of the processional route, the golden throne that represented the authority of the monarch and thus of the government itself, was Pugin's own design. The arrangement of the Lords' chamber around royal ceremonial formed a secular parallel to Pugin's arrangement of church designs around liturgy. He made the comparison himself, writing that the veneration of sacred symbols in churches 'is paralleled in temporal matters by the external respect shown to the throne in the House of Peers'.[14] He continued: 'Sacred imagery is a noble field for the exercise of the highest powers of art; and painting and sculpture when devoted to the service of the Church, are calculated to improve and elevate religious feeling of the nation to a surprising degree'. By analogy, the art and decoration of the chamber would likewise animate patriotism. Pugin went on to lay out his theory for the decoration of royal palaces, such as the Palace of Westminster:

> Surely the long succession of our kings – their noble achievements, – the honourable badges and charges that they bore, – would form subjects which would naturally suggest themselves for the decorations of various halls and apartments. How truly grand and national would a building thus designed and ornamented appear, where not only the general character, but every detail, was expressive of the dignity of the country, and an illustration of its history![15]

Just as the design of sacred buildings was meant to always hold religion before the mind, the civic building was meant to inspire politicians with reminders of history. For the House of Lords, in addition to Pugin's heraldic decoration, a series of frescoes was planned on themes from medieval British history. The introduction of frescoes was not Barry's or Pugin's idea, but that of a commission of artistic experts set up to oversee the introduction of fine art into the palace. William Dyce and Prince Albert, the leaders of the commission, were particularly excited about contemporary experiments being conducted by Bavarian artists in reviving the technique of fresco. A fresco cycle on British history, they felt, would put the palace on par with European trends and encourage British prowess in what was regarded as the highest genre of painting.

Pugin was ultimately pleased with this plan. He also admired the German fresco revival, especially the work of the Nazarenes, Germanic artists who sought to channel the spirit of Christianity by returning to the style and techniques of early Flemish and Italian oil painters. Pugin felt that the Nazarenes were reviving true principles in painting, and he had commissioned one of them, the Swiss artist Eduard Hauser, to create the Doom painting over the chancel arch at Cheadle.

The artists selected for the mural cycle at the Houses of Parliament were the British painters most strongly influenced by the Nazarene example. Pugin considered them to be among the leaders of British art. He thought William Dyce's work was excellent, and J R Herbert was a close friend who would paint Pugin's portrait and later convert to Catholicism at Pugin's urging.

Pugin's taste in modern art was surprisingly avant-garde, and he counted a number of painters among his friends. The painters Pugin liked best were using medieval sources as inspiration for modern painting, just as Pugin himself was doing with architecture and decoration. Besides Dyce and Herbert, William Etty was also a friend who came to stay at The Grange, although his controversial paintings of nudes against brightly coloured backgrounds were distant from Pugin's other expressed artistic tastes. Pugin sometimes visited the Royal Academy Summer Exhibition, and it was there in 1849 that he saw the first painting by Millais to bear the mysterious 'PRB' monogram of the Pre-Raphaelite Brotherhood. 'That's going to be the man', he exclaimed; 'He has the medieval spirit in him'.[16] Pugin himself exhibited four watercolours at the Royal Academy that summer, including a striking bird's-eye view of The Grange and St Augustine's. He hoped to be elected ARA, but the Academy did not select him, and the hanging committee may have skied his pictures.

One of the principles that Pugin espoused in art was the avoidance of overly secular subject matter. He was scathing about the portraiture that dominated the Royal Academy exhibitions: 'What loads of ill-painted faces line the rooms ... curly-headed boys with hoops; boarding school misses feeding kittens ... sprucely dressed men looking inconceivably silly; ladies playing with poodles and fans, or vacantly staring ... all are to be found to the life'.[17] Art, he felt, should turn the mind towards God. Even portraiture could do this by showing subjects holding rosary beads or including a crucifix in the background.

The other major principle that Pugin championed for modern Christian art was anatomical correctness – he believed that the emotive distortions of medieval art came from a lack of knowledge. Anatomy was a form of modern technical knowledge, just as iron construction was. Both were required if art and architecture were not to mimic the past, but to be truly of their time. Once again prefiguring the rhetoric of the Modernist Movement, Pugin declared that art must reflect the 'system' of its moment.[18] As with so many of Pugin's tastes, anatomically correct sculpture became a defining feature of the Victorian Gothic Revival. The presence of such art is one way that a Victorian Gothic building can be immediately recognised as a product of the 19th century, no matter how otherwise archaeologically accurate and medieval-looking it may be.

Pugin was not a fine artist. He was an excellent draftsman, but his figure drawing was always weak. Oil painting and sculpture were two media in which he did not himself dabble, and as such, his theories about art were not as fully developed as his philosophy of architecture. In *Apology*, he insisted that style did not matter in painting and sculpture; the only essential was that Christian principles of devotion, majesty, and repose were observed.[19]

Thus Pugin could praise Greek sculptures as 'grand expressions of nature', and professed appreciation for neo-Classical sculptures by Flaxman, while still condemning Flaxman's use of 'indecent' Classical costume.[20] Pugin's taste in art was one of the few places in which his position in the chronology of art history was revealed; his taste in sculpture was essentially of the Regency, preferring elegant figures and dramatic settings.

Reforming art education

And yet it was study of casts of Greek and Roman sculpture and an over-emphasis on the nude that Pugin roundly condemned in the Royal Academy Schools. The examples studied by students, Pugin predictably felt, should be medieval. On his own initiative, he made great progress towards compiling a national collection of medieval casts for student study. He cleverly used his position as Superintendent of Wood-Carving at the Palace of Westminster in order to do so. He had it written into the terms of his contract with Barry that he was authorised to collect casts and actual medieval artefacts for the inspiration of the wood carvers. In that role, he procured hundreds of casts and specimens for the artisans working on the new Parliament buildings. Hundreds of examples were surely much more than necessary for the Parliament project; however, it was his plan from the first 'that they may be united in one great collection when they are done with & they may form the commencement of a great National Gallery – of antient art'.[21]

In keeping with his plan, when the collection was no longer needed for the wood carvers, it was transferred to the new Architectural Museum, one of the South Kensington institutions set up after the Great Exhibition to educate the nation's designers.

Ultimately Pugin's collection would serve exactly the function he wanted it to: it was highly important in laying the educational groundwork for the Gothic Revival. Even Ruskin would come to regard the collection as an important national resource, donating his own casts of Venice to supplement the Pugin casts. That the Gothic Revival could go from conditions in which very few practitioners had a knowledge of correct medieval forms, to one in which only 30 years later most practising architects had a thorough under-standing of Gothic design amounted to a substantial transformation of the art education system. The emphasis had shifted to deep archaeological knowledge (which Cockerell had also promoted in his role as Professor at the Royal Academy). By the 1860s, the medieval was treated on a level with the Classical. Examples of true medieval building were much closer to

The Architectural Museum at Canon's Row, where many of Pugin's casts were deposited shortly after his death. [© Victoria and Albert Museum, London]

hand than the Continental canon of Classical and Renaissance building, and young architects without the means for foreign travel could study them closely. The study of medieval buildings taught these students how the architectural details captured by Pugin's casts related to the broader whole. Pugin's collection would eventually end up as part of the Victoria and Albert Museum.

Pugin had long promoted the reform of design education, calling for the teaching of modern manufacturing techniques and a focus on principles rather than style. In 1845, he wrote to *The Builder* that the national School of Design should teach students to be 'not mere imitators of any style, but men imbued with a thorough knowledge of the history, wants, climate, and customs of our country; who would combine all the spirit of the mediaeval architects and the beauties of the old Christian artists, with the practical improvements of our times'.[22] In his *Apology* he wrote that an ideal architectural education would consist of the study of Christian religion, history, liturgy, vernacular building traditions and natural resources.[23] These statements gave insight into Pugin's architectural ideal. The young architects whom Pugin hoped would transform the Victorian city into a Gothic utopia, would need not only to understand technical aspects of building, especially as it related to various local conditions, but also the social and cultural contexts to which their designs had to respond. It was essential, Pugin felt, that architects understand the complex way a building's impact on its users was influenced by cultural factors, because the purpose of the built environment was to shape society. Pugin was by no means the only voice calling for the reform of design education; in some sense that was the entire aim of the Great Exhibition and of the new institutions in South Kensington. But Pugin's voice was an influential one, helping to stoke the fires of change. His concerns would work their way into curricula via a growing emphasis on architectural history as the 19th century progressed, ultimately reaching its height in the writings of William Lethaby and Banister Fletcher.[24]

Critical reception of the Lords' Chamber

With the opening of the chamber of the House of Lords on 15 April 1847, Queen Victoria became the first monarch to sit on the golden throne, and every year afterwards she would travel to the new palace to receive the people's representatives and form a government. The design of the chamber was popular with critics and the public, although the queen herself was rumoured to consider it too ornate.[25] The opinion that the chamber was over-gilded and ostentatious would dog Pugin's reputation for years, especially during the 20th century. When the architect Giles Gilbert Scott first saw the interiors of the palace in 1905, he recorded in his sketchbook, 'There is far too much gilding and varnish ... The effect produced upon me one of abject depression'.[26] When he later went on to rebuild the House of Commons chamber after its destruction during the Second World War, he would omit the gilding and varnish he had found so oppressive.

For many of us raised with the Modernist image tradition, photographs of Pugin's interiors seem to back up Scott's assessment. However, Pugin's architecture always looks better in real life. One reason for this is that photographs compress the incredible richness of detail in interiors such as the House of Lords or Cheadle, so that whether in colour or black and white, they appear so busy as to become difficult to read. They seem to overwhelm the senses with fuss. One must remember when viewing such a photograph that in actuality the detail is spread over significant three-dimensional space, distinguished by projecting and receding forms. Furthermore, each detail, rather than appearing at the small scale of the photograph, exists in reality at a more natural human scale. That is one thing that Pugin did exceedingly well – the scale of his detail, fittings and furnishings was always right. One of Pugin's main objections to the Gothic of Horace Walpole's Strawberry Hill was its disregard for rational scale – fire grates with tiny battlements and arrow slits a few inches high infuriated him.[27] Pugin never used these devices. That is part of the reason his buildings often felt more like their medieval predecessors – the scale and density of detail, regardless of the level of ornamental profusion, sits comfortably.

Commerce: Pugin as luxury brand

The profusion of decorative art that Pugin created for the Palace of Westminster, whether one considers it to be glittering excess or a powerful aesthetic expression, was made possible by the Victorian industrial and commercial system of which Pugin was a part. It is easy to think of Pugin as a romantic outsider, a zealous utopian whose clients belonged to a minority group intent on reshaping society from the outside. And in some ways this is perfectly accurate. But Pugin was many things, and it is important to remember that he always operated his design business through the London commercial world. He was a product of London – his father had run a design business, and he had his own start in set design and furniture manufacture. Although his first furniture business failed, he was ultimately a successful businessman, much more so than his father had been. He was able to live in style, build a church, buy a boat, support six children, travel for months on the Continent, collect medieval art, ride first class on the railway, and support a substantial programme of charitable giving.

For 12 of the 17 years that he practised architecture, Pugin kept lodgings at Cheyne Walk in Chelsea. He designed a Gothic showroom for the decorator John Crace's premises in Wigmore Street that was expressly dedicated to the display of Gothic products mostly designed by Pugin himself. Hardman & Co sold hundreds of his metalwork designs each year, many of which were stock Pugin-designed items marketed to the general public. And Pugin planned a show-stopping display – the Medieval Court – for the greatest trade fair of all, the Great Exhibition of 1851.

To some extent his design business operated like a modern luxury brand – his wild artistic persona and radical social ideas adding to the mystique of his products. Pugin was deeply sincere in his social and religious convictions, but he believed that Christian art would promote Christianity in all contexts, and one such setting was the fashionable drawing room via the London shop. Although his architectural services were mostly engaged by Catholic clients who shared his ideals, the majority of his decorating

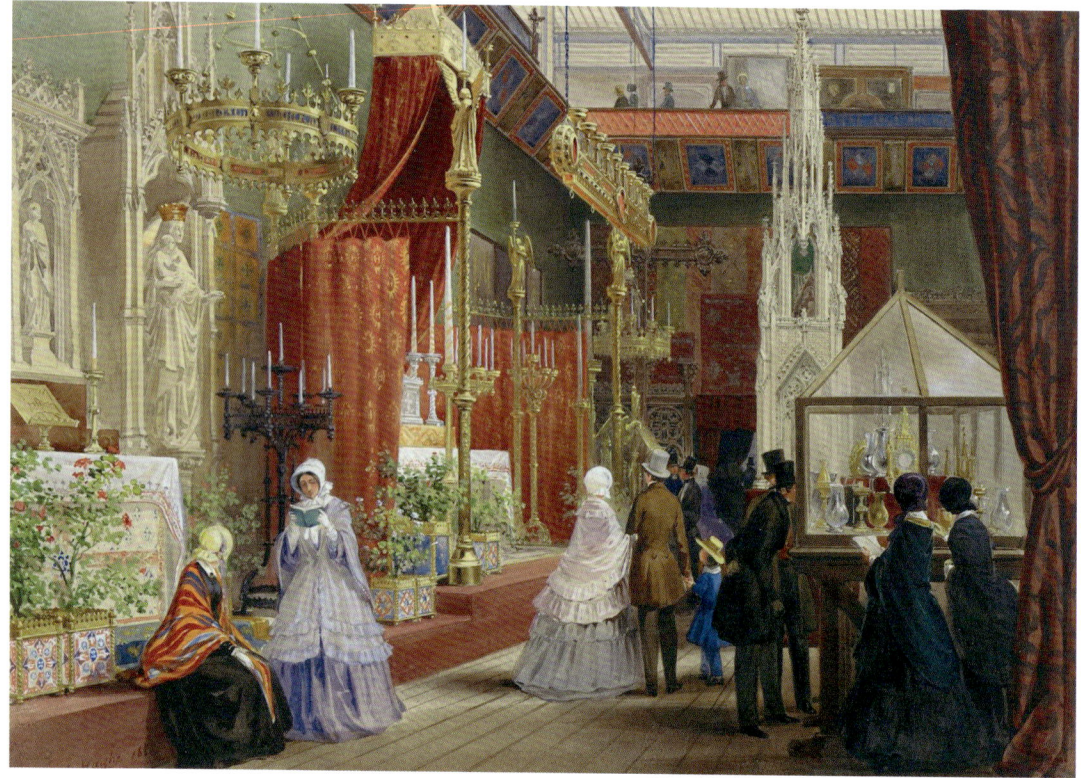

The Medieval Court at the Great Exhibition. [Public Domain]

business – the sales of stained glass, light fixtures, tableware, andirons, and hinges by Hardman, of Minton tea services and flower pots, of the Gothic furniture from Crace's Pugin showroom – must have been to well-to-do Anglican shoppers who wanted something beautiful and slightly edgy to donate to their church or to decorate their houses. Thanks largely to Pugin's own efforts, by the later 1840s, the Gothic Revival was increasingly popular. During his lifetime it was never completely mainstream, but after all, that is the ideal market condition for a luxury brand. Consumers want their purchases to attract notice, to make a statement.

One should not understand this to mean that Pugin was a hypocrite. He was anything but that. The search for better social conditions came through religion, the transformation of social institutions, and the rejection of industrialist abuses. Pugin declared at the opening of St Chad's that 'never shall I rest satisfied till I see the cross raised high above every chimney in Birmingham, and hear the sound of St Chad's bells drowning the steam whistle'.[28] He believed that Christian art would help to temper the cruelty of industry. He was not calling for violent social revolution, which terrified him. He was deeply radical, but his ideas about how to effect change went down a different track. He knew that Christianity is a much more subtle, much more powerful thing, infiltrating through unexpected corridors. 'We hail the present feelings of admiration for Anglo-Catholic antiquity', he wrote, 'as a probable means of eventually restoring the faith, and not as an abstract question of art and taste'.[29]

Manufacturing

Some later Victorian artists advocated a return to medieval handicraft, but that was never Pugin's vision for society. He never rejected technology; he always merely proposed to change what was manufactured within the current system. The machine was a means of improving the conditions of labour, of increasing productivity by decreasing time wasted on tedious

Ceramic plate decorated by lithographic process. [© Victoria and Albert Museum, London]

tasks, and of improving safety in operations such as cutting and heavy lifting.[30] Machines allowed the artisans who were among Pugin's dearest friends to put more Christian art into the world at a faster rate. This was not mass manufacturing in the sense of repetitively producing identical products at rapid speed. Instead, Pugin's manufactories operated on the workshop principle, with artisans specialising in one operation such as machine engraving or enamelling so that they could quickly apply their skills to the production of individually designed pieces.[31]

Pugin believed the steam engine was a marvel that facilitated the rapid technological development of his own time. He was conscious of being part of a 'generation of innovators'.[32] As such, he was quick to adopt new techniques – Minton's encaustic tiles, advances in sanitation and lighting, new methods of stained-glass production. He himself even helped to pioneer a manufacturing process: lithographic printing on ceramic. Hardly backward-looking, the Medieval Court was a showcase of new techniques. Alongside expensive individually crafted works of art, such as the towering stone baptismal font now at St Augustine's, Ramsgate, and the great wardrobe now in the V&A, there were mass-produced ceramics, some decorated using the new lithographic process, which were sold to exhibition visitors in large quantities.[33]

Alongside these wares were Gothic designs for all aspects of modern life. In a way, the Medieval Court paralleled the 'city of the tomorrow' displays that would captivate audiences at later world's fairs. It was one of the most popular exhibits in the Crystal Palace because visitors could imagine the ideal Gothic city of steam.

The soul of the cities

Pugin laid out his vision for the future of the city in his 1843 book, *An Apology for the Revival of Christian Architecture*. The book addressed the way the Gothic Revival could tackle its final and greatest challenge – transforming the Victorian city. The early Victorian city was a place of uncontrolled growth alongside Dickensian poverty, of vast engineering projects for bridges, tunnels and railways, huge shipyards, new sewers, public streetlights. Its dense soot and the noxious fumes from coal fires, gas lighting, and clusters of smoking factories made it polluted and unhealthy. Floods of new arrivals from the country and wealth from industrialisation and global trade fuelled a building boom – hotels, asylums, civic buildings, railway stations, houses, colleges, schools and countless other buildings rose at a rate never before seen. Many of these building types were innovations. London was the largest of all such cities – a world metropolis and capital of global commerce. The Victorians were struggling to control this smoking dragon, to make sure that its vast energy was turned to good rather than destruction. Pugin charged

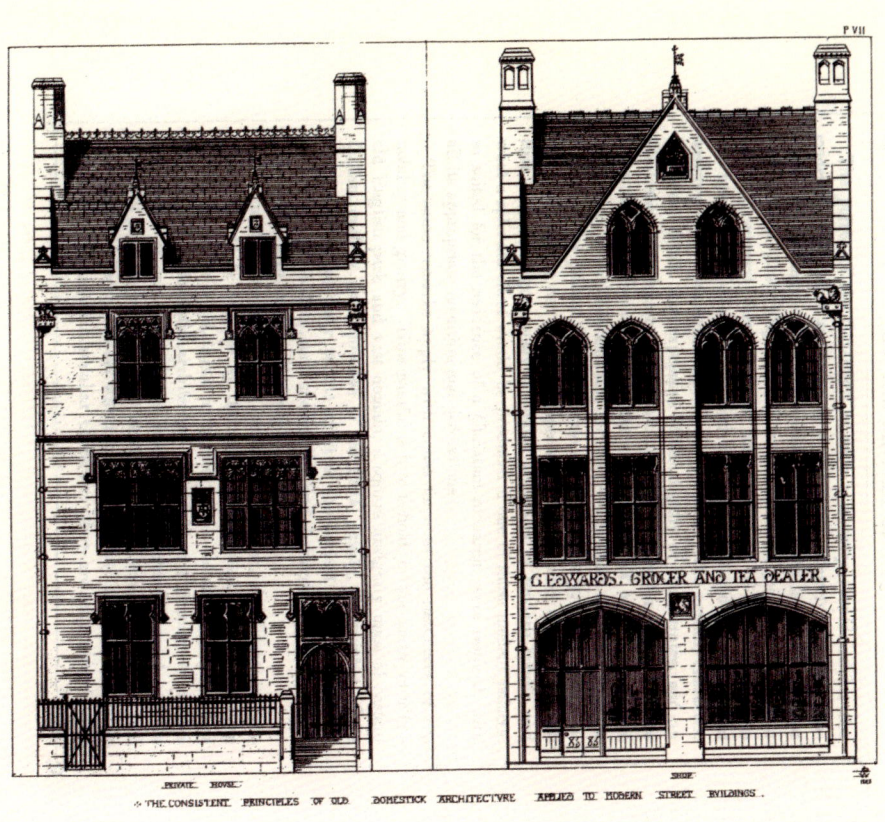

Ideal town houses illustrated in *An Apology for the Revival of Gothic Architecture*.
[Public Domain]

bravely into the fray, trumpeting what he saw as the one solution: the clarion call to compassion and charity represented in Christian art.

It was easy enough to see how the Gothic Revival might work in the countryside by adding great halls to country houses and erecting stone churches for religious revival, but the buildings and problems of the modern city had no clear medieval precedent. Pugin, however, showed how it was not direct precedent that mattered, but the application of true principles to modern design problems. *Apology*, though somewhat rambling in structure, successfully predicted a number of key features of the High Victorian city.

The secret to the city house, Pugin said, was variety not unity. The long rows of identical stucco fronts, the imposition of false symmetry, and the

Houses in Midleton, Ireland, likely designed by Pugin. [Richard Butler]

disguising of functional features such as chimneys were inharmonious developments. He praised early 18th-century houses in Queen Square and Red Lion Square for 'high roofs, bold overhanging cornices [that deflected water], and good dormers'.[34] Pugin knew his readers would be shocked to find such a staunch Gothicist defending early Georgian design, but it was only their decoration, he wrote, that was bad. Any architecture in which the principles were sound, was better than that which was impractical or ill-constructed. The ideal, though, was of course Gothic. He illustrated two ideal town houses of his own design.

They were terrace houses that focused on structural expression and fitness for climate. They had pitched roofs, tall chimneys, and the large-windowed shopfronts of the ground floor were spanned by pointed arches. One house even presented a gable front directly to the street. In this way they anticipated the type of house that would become the London standard; the gabled, brick house that would come to define whole tracts of the West End.

Although he worked out some of these ideas in his parsonage designs, presenting a narrow gable end to the street on at least one occasion, it was in Ireland that he seems to have had his only chance to realise a true town house design. Two stone houses in Midleton, County Cork, are very similar to the ideal town houses he illustrated in *Apology*, down to the treatment of the transoms, wide shop windows under pointed arches, and gabled dormers.

They cannot be firmly attributed to Pugin because the records of Lord Midleton's Irish estates were left in confusion at the time of his death in 1848, but it seems likely that they were designed in 1847 at a time when Pugin was executing a number of other buildings for Lord Midleton.[35]

Pugin loathed grand gestures of urban Classicism. He attacked Euston Station for not reflecting the reality of its function. He claimed it was merely a grand masonry temple front hung on a shed, its mammoth gateway a tasteless advertising gimmick serving no functional purpose. (A counter-argument might be that the gateway both served as a landmark to help passengers find their way to the station and also masterfully symbolised the purpose of the station itself as a gateway to London.) Modern classicists, Pugin insisted, had lost sight of the constructive and functional principles that governed the works of ancient Classical designers. If Vitruvius, for instance, could somehow come back to life to behold Euston Station, 'Vitruvius would spew'.[36]

What Pugin believed the railways needed was honest engineering. Simple battering and pointed arches would do for railway embankments and bridges. Instead of expensive stone temple waiting rooms, railway companies should provide simple constructive shelters. During a trip to Germany, the Mannheim steam engines smoking and whistling under their iron canopy had captured Pugin's imagination, and he wrote to Charles Barry calling the new stations on the Mannheim to Strasbourg line the 'best modern architecture I have seen'.[37]

England was yet to see the canopies of iron and glass that would define its greatest stations – Isambard Kingdom Brunel's Paddington would not be completed until two years after Pugin's death. However, Pugin already saw the Gothic potential in constructional ironwork. One can only imagine that he would have loved St Pancras, with its pointed wrought-iron roof wrapped by the heavy Gothic masonry of the Midland Grand Hotel. Hardly believing it to be contradictory, as some Modernist critics have claimed it is, he would have said that the two elements of train shed and hotel fit their functions perfectly – the vast train shed providing economical Gothic shelter and the hotel comfortable Gothic accommodation. St Pancras was the ultimate expression of the Puginian vision for the city, designed by Pugin's devoted follower, George Gilbert Scott. However, Pugin would not live to see his vision fulfilled. The Houses of Parliament represented a new paradigm of modern urbanism, but they would remain the only major secular London building to which Pugin contributed. He was never invited to design a London terrace house or a railway station.

Mannheim Railway Station. [Public Domain]

Heidelberg Railway Station. [Public Domain]

In the end, Pugin succumbed to other problems of the modern city – exhaustion, drugs, and mental illness. Pugin's doctors had prescribed mercury, a drug whose effects they did not properly understand, for a recurring ailment relating to his eyes. This almost certainly contributed to his final decline. There has been much speculation about the cause and extent of his illness, but whatever the case, in 1852 Pugin was driven to collapse and a flash of mental instability, before his sudden death at the age of 40.

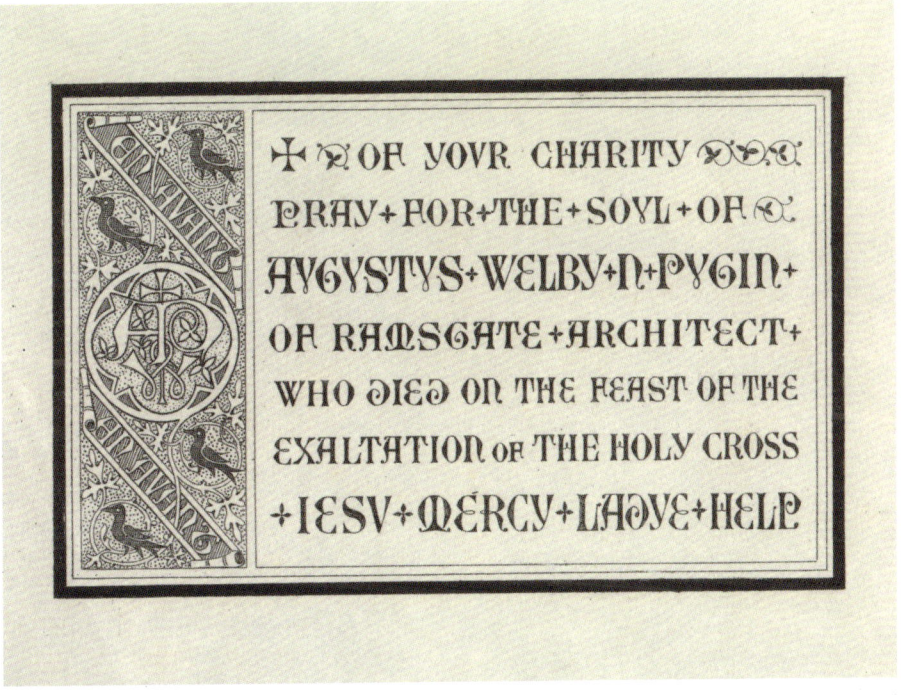

Funeral card for A Welby Pugin. [Yale Center for British Art, Paul Mellon Collection B1977.14.20667]

5   En avant

Pugin's death was completely unexpected. Poignantly, the young architects W E Nesfield and Norman Shaw, who would become architectural stars of the next generation, arrived at The Grange to try to meet their hero, only to find that he had died a few days previously. They ended up attending his funeral. The vast stream of projects in education, manufacturing and architecture that had flowed from Pugin's pencil for the previous two decades was suddenly cut off. Some would be finished by his teenaged son Edward, who leapt into architecture at a young age, just as his father had done. Edward and all his brothers would practice architecture in a style derived from the work of their father. The Roman Catholic institutions that had patronised Augustus Pugin would often stay loyal to the family – Ushaw College, for instance, had a Pugin as its architect for nearly 100 years.

Loyalty to the Pugins was also strong in Ireland, where Catholic priests, many trained at Maynooth, would invite Edward to design new churches, including the lacy cathedral of Cobh.

In the decades following his death, the Gothic Revival thrived, and Pugin was hailed as an architectural hero and the founder of a movement. Although the occasional critic would point to flaws in his work, his reputation would remain consistently strong throughout the 19th century. Enthusiasm wavered, taste shifted, but Pugin's name never fell into obscurity – there was no getting around the fact that whatever one thought of his designs, he was one of the most significant architects of the Victorian era.

In the early 20th century, church architects especially continued to regard him highly. Influential British church designer Charles Nicholson took it for granted that Pugin was one of the founders of modern ecclesiastical art.[1] Architect Ralph Adams Cram, who would transform a number of American university campuses into Gothic wonderlands during the first four decades of the 20th century, had a statue of Pugin carved for the mantelpiece of his New York office. Architecture critic Charles Marriott wrote in the 1920s that without Pugin there would have been no modern British architecture.[2] The low ebb of Pugin's reputation came in the 1940s and 1950s, when he was seen as the epitome of dark and dreary Victorian design. And yet, even then there

Ushaw College Chapel, incorporating fittings designed by Pugin for the previous chapel. [Author]

Cobh Cathedral, designed by Edward Pugin. [Author]

were champions of his work, even if they were occasionally tongue-in-cheek – poet John Betjeman, artist Cecil Beaton, writer Evelyn Waugh, curator Kenneth Clark, began the process of reviving the revivalists.

As architectural tastes shifted, Pugin's ideas remained important. Pugin's linkage of morality and architecture helped to lay the rhetorical foundation of 20th-century Modernism, with its resounding claim that the world's social ills could be solved by a combination of planning, technology and aesthetics. The architecture critic Nikolaus Pevsner would claim that two key Modernist ideas had a direct lineage from Pugin's writing: the concept of honest construction and the concept of designing the façade of a building to express its plan.[3] It was Pevsner's pupil, Phoebe Stanton, who wrote the first modern study of Pugin's architecture in 1971.[4] However, Pevsner's view of Pugin was somewhat flawed. Pevsner wanted to present architectural history as a narrative of progress in which increasingly rational architecture pointed inevitably towards 20th-century Modernism. But over the course of his career

opposite above: Arch at a Yale University residential college, carved with the balance from Pugin's *Contrasts* and completed in 2017. [Author]

opposite: The famous illustration of the balance from Pugin's *Contrasts*, showing modern architecture to be less substantial than the medieval Gothic. [Public Domain]

he prevaricated about Pugin – Pugin's ideas about ornament did not fit with Pevsner's own taste; Pugin's concern with provoking feelings and spiritual experience was an aspect of human psychology that International Modernism hoped to ignore. Pevsner was trying to make Pugin into something that he was not. That Pugin is no longer considered a proto-Modernist has more to do with the breakdown of Pevsner's deterministic narrative of 20th-century architecture than a disbelief in Pugin's contribution to modern architectural thought.

Outside the world of criticism, Pugin had always been respected: Gothic Revivalists and church architects such as Giles Gilbert Scott and Ninian Comper, although they sometimes felt his work overly ornamented, regarded him as part of their intellectual foundation; congregations cared lovingly for their Pugin churches; and generations of Britons regarded the Houses of Parliament as the ultimate expression of Britishness. In the second half of the 20th century, the Victorian Society helped to stem the tide of destruction that befell Victorian buildings after the Second World War, and the small but mighty Pugin Society arose to help preserve his buildings and encourage Pugin studies.

By the late 20th century, Pugin was once again a name that many people knew. His cultural relevance today suddenly seems enormous. A generation raised on Harry Potter revels in the Gothic Revival aesthetic. Steampunk and Victoriana subcultures flourish. Among some groups, there is increased interest in the local, the sustainable, and perhaps even a whiff of Pugin's self-righteousness. Architects continue to build in Gothic Revival. The new colleges at Yale University, for instance, built in a Gothic Revival style, have an illustration from Pugin's book *Contrasts* carved in stone on one of the spandrels – forever recording the building's debt to his ideas.

Today's historians take it for granted that Pugin was one of the most important architectural theorists of the Victorian world.

Most of Pugin's buildings still stand. Many of his churches, because they are Roman Catholic, are open every day. It is still possible to make the pilgrimage to Cheadle, as so many Victorian architects did, to see Pugin's famous church. One can stroll along the cliffs at Ramsgate, where Pugin's banner still flaps above the tower of The Grange – now owned by the Landmark Trust and let to holiday-makers – and one can visit St Augustine's, newly refreshed with help from the Heritage Lottery Fund. Tour guides shepherd tourists through the golden splendour of the House of Lords (or you can watch the monarch there each year on television). For those interested in learning more about Pugin, there is much to read and much to see.

Notes

Introduction

1   Trappes-Lomax, M 1932 *Pugin: A Medieval Victorian*. London: Sheed & Ward, 56.

2   Hyland, G J 2018 *Beyond 'Puginism'*. Reading: Spire, 45.

3   A short biography of Pugin with more detail than I am able to give here, giving fuller scope to his non-architectural design activities and to his personal life, can be found in Alexandra Wedgwood's entry on Pugin in the *Oxford Dictionary of National Biography*.

4   A collection of these early measured drawings survives at the Yale Center for British Art, New Haven, USA.

5   The information in these paragraphs is from Wedgwood, A 2008 'Pugin, Augustus Welby Northmore', *Oxford Dictionary of National Biography*, online.

6   Levine, N 2010 *Modern Architecture: Representation and Reality*. New Haven: Yale, 116–148.

7   Pugin, A W N 1841 *The True Principles of Pointed or Christian Architecture*. London: John Weale (facsim edn Spire 2003).

8   Ibid, 1.

9   Wedgwood, A 1994 'The New Palace of Westminster' in Atterbury, P and Wainwright, C (eds) *Pugin: A Gothic Passion*. London: Yale, 219.

10 Pugin, A W N 1844 *Glossary of Ecclesiastical Ornament and Costume*. London: Henry Bohn, iii.

11 Lesser, W 2017 *You Say to Brick: The Life of Louis Kahn*. New York: Farrar, Straus and Giroux, 5.

12 Stanton, P 1971 *Pugin*. New York: Viking.

1 The house of God

1   Betjeman, J 2014 *Lovely Bits of Old England: Selected Writings from* The Telegraph. London: Aurum, ix.

2   Stanton, P 1971 *Pugin*. New York: Viking, 60.

3   Saint, A 2005 'St Chad's, Birmingham: Not so very foreign?' in *True Principles* **3**:2, 70.

4   Hill, R 2007 *God's Architect: Pugin and the Building of Romantic Britain*. London: Penguin, 238.

5   Pierre Patte's 1777 edition of Blondel's *Cours d'architecture* already contained a fairly sophisticated understanding of Gothic construction that was developed rapidly over the following decades.

6   Alexander, M 2007 *Medievalism: The Middle Ages in Modern England*. London: Yale, 79.

7   Pugin, A C 1821–c 1825 *Specimens of Gothic Architecture*. London: J Taylor; Pugin A C 1838–40 *Examples of Gothic Architecture*. London: Henry Bohn, to name just two of his projects.

8   The Sarum Use is a variant of the Roman Rite, the mainstream worship practice of the Roman Catholic Church, not a

distinct Rite such as the Ambrosian
Rite or the Mozarabic Rite. The clearest
explanation of the Sarum Use and its
relationship to Pugin's architecture is
provided in Hyland, G J 2018 *Beyond
'Puginism'*. Reading: Spire.

9 The phrase 'religious technology' to
describe Pugin's concept of a Gothic
Revival system is a slightly modified
version of the Australian scholar Karen
Burn's useful concept of Pugin's system
as 'moral technology'. Brittain-Catlin,
T, DeMeyer, J, and Bressani, M (eds)
2016 *Gothic Revival Worldwide: A W N
Pugin's Global Influence*. Leuven: Leuven
Univ, KADOC-Artes, 134.

10 Pugin, A W N 1838 'Lectures on ecclesiastical architecture: Lecture the First'
reprinted in *True Principles* **5**:2, 92.

11 For an excellent discussion of this
concept, from which I borrow the phrase
'architecture of affect', see Whyte, W
2017 *Unlocking the Church: The Lost Secrets
of Victorian Sacred Space*. Oxford: Oxford
University Press.

12 Pugin to Bloxam, 26 September 1843
(?), Belcher, M (ed) 2003 *The Collected
Letters of A W N Pugin* **2**. Oxford: Oxford
University Press, 111.

13 Blondel, Perrault, Ledoux, Schinkel, and
Robert Owen all explore this idea. For
a discussion of Pugin's place in broader
architectural theory, see Watkin, D
1977 *Morality and Architecture*. Chicago:
Chicago University Press, 17–23.

14 Richardson, D S 1970 *Gothic Revival
Architecture in Ireland*. PhD dissertation, Yale
University, 257, although the attribution to
Pugin has been questioned: O'Donnell, R
1995 'The Pugins in Ireland', in Atterbury,
P (ed) 1995 *A W N Pugin: Master of Gothic
Revival*. London: Yale, 141.

15 Stanton *Pugin*, 39.

16 A phrase Pugin famously used to
describe the Houses of Parliament, see
Wedgwood, A 1994 'The New Palace
of Westminster', in Atterbury, P and
Wainwright, C (eds) *Pugin: A Gothic
Passion*. London: Yale, 221.

17 Stanton *Pugin*, 41.

18 The screen at St Chad's, Birmingham,
was designed after Macclesfield's.

19 Pugin's use of screens is a large and
complex topic. He would devote an
entire book to the subject. An excellent
analysis of his use of screens and their
meaning is found in Hyland *Beyond
'Puginism'*, 15–42.

20 The Latin is from Psalm 26, 'Lord, I
have loved the habitation of thy house:
and the place where thine honour
dwelleth'; Pugin, A W N 1841 *Contrasts:
or a Parallel between the Noble Edifices
of the Middle Ages and Corresponding
Buildings of the Present Day: Shewing the
Present Decay of Taste*. London: Charles
Dolman, 4–5.

21 The locomotive quotation is from a
letter from Pugin to David Charles Read,
14 January 1841, quoted in Belcher, M (ed)
2001 *The Collected Letters of A W N Pugin* **1**.
Oxford: Oxford University Press, 194.

22 Anon 1848 *Description of the College Chapel
of St Cuthbert, Ushaw*.

23 Hyland G J 2014 *The Architectural Works of
A W N Pugin: A Catalogue*. Reading: Spire,
35.

24 This description of Pugin's ideal church
comes from Gerard Hyland, who has
gathered and analysed the data on what
Pugin built, providing great insight
into his architecture as it was actually
practiced. Hyland *The Architectural Works
of A W N Pugin*, 27–34.

25 Pugin *Contrasts*; Pugin *True Principles*.

26 Pugin, A W N 1844 *Glossary of Ecclesiastical Ornament and Costume*. London: Henry Bohn. These books have all been digitised and, at the time of publication, are available as free downloads from The Internet Archive (www.archive.org).

27 Belcher, M (ed) 2015 *The Collected Letters of A W N Pugin* **5**. Oxford: Oxford University Press, xii.

28 Fisher, M 2013 *St Giles Church, Cheadle*. Stoke-on-Trent: Urban Vision, 3.

29 Pugin to Shrewsbury, 31 March 1841? in Belcher *Collected Letters* **1**, 226.

30 That is, 'Gate of heaven!' Quoted in Stanton *Pugin*, 108.

31 Pugin, A W N 1841 *The True Principles of Pointed or Christian Architecture*. London: John Weale (facsim edn Spire 2003), 34.

32 Ibid, 4.

33 For a study of Pugin's stained glass, see Shepherd, S 2009 *The Stained Glass of A W N Pugin*, Reading: Spire.

34 Pugin *True Principles*, 1.

35 Pugin, A W N 1843 *An Apology for the Revival of Christian Architecture in England*. London: John Weale, 21.

36 Quoted in Horner, L and Hunter, G 2000 *A Flint Seaside Church: St Augustine's Abbey Church, Ramsgate*. Ramsgate: Pugin Society, 10.

37 Pugin *True Principles*, 56.

38 O'Donnell 'The Pugins in Ireland', 142.

39 Richardson *Gothic Revival Architecture in Ireland*, 291.

40 Ibid, 276.

41 Ibid, 283.

42 Pugin *Apology*, 23, n13.

43 Richardson *Gothic Revival Architecture in Ireland*, 287.

44 Bremner, A (ed) 2012 *Ecclesiology Abroad: The British Empire and Beyond*. Studies in Victorian Architecture & Design **4**. London: Victorian Society.

45 *The Tablet*, Sept 1848, quoted in Andrews, B 1994 'Pugin in Australia' in Atterbury and Wainwright 1994 *Pugin: A Gothic Passion*, 246.

46 Hill *God's Architect*, 360.

47 Wedgwood, A (ed) 1988? 'Pugin in His Home': A Memoir by J H Powell. Ramsgate: Pugin Society, 13.

48 I owe the example of Littlemore and any analysis of it to William Whyte's *Unlocking the Church*, which does more than can be done here to illuminate the architectural world in which Pugin worked, and for perhaps the first time tells the story of Pugin, the Ecclesiologists, and indeed all of the other church builders of the period as a single narrative. It is striking especially for demonstrating just how much of Pugin's ideology was not his own invention, but rather belonged to a broad consensus of like-minded clerics and scholars. On Pugin and Littlemore, Whyte, W 2017 *Unlocking the Church: The Lost Secrets of Victorian Sacred Space*. Oxford: Oxford University Press, 8.

49 Whyte *Unlocking the Church*, 93.

50 Hill *God's Architect*, 1.

51 Stamp, G 2015 *Gothic for the Steam Age*. London: Aurum, 41–2.

52 O'Donnell 'The Pugins in Ireland', 152.

53 Coffman, P 2016 'Meanings of Gothic in Atlantic Canada: c 1840–1890'; and McNair, S 2016 'Richard Upjohn and the Gothic in Antebellum Alabama' in Brittain-Catlin, T, DeMeyer, J, and Bressani, M (eds) 2016 *Gothic Revival Worldwide: A W N Pugin's Global Influence*. Leuven: Leuven Univ, KADOC-Artes.

54 The most thorough exploration of Pugin's influence abroad, with two chapters devoted to Bethune, is Brittain-Catlin *et al Gothic Revival Worldwide*.

55 Basciano J 2016 'Notre-Dame de Bonsecours (1840–1844) and the Catholic context of the French Gothic Revival' in Brittain-Catlin *et al Gothic Revival Worldwide*.

56 Hill *God's Architect*, 270.

57 These proportions were worked out by Stanton: *Pugin*, 111–12.

58 Pugin, A W N 1843 *The Present State of Ecclesiastical Architecture in England*. London: Charles Dolman, 59 n.

59 Hyland, G J 2018 *Beyond 'Puginism'*. Reading: Spire, 44.

60 Pugin *True Principles*, 63.

61 Hyland *Beyond 'Puginism'*, 45–6.

62 This analysis is taken from Hyland *Beyond 'Puginism'*, which sheds great light on Pugin's late churches.

63 Ibid, 45.

64 O'Donnell, R 1994 'Pugin as church architect' in Atterbury and Wainwright 1994 *Pugin: A Gothic Passion*, 77.

65 Pugin, A W N 1849 *Floriated Ornament*. London: Henry Bohn, introduction (no page numbers).

66 Wedgwood '*Pugin in His Home*', 27.

67 Pugin to John Morris, 1 January 1851, in Belcher *Collected Letters* **5**, 4.

68 Webster, J 2011 'A W N Pugin's Grange at Ramsgate'. *True Principles* **4**:2, 191–2.

2 The house of man

1 Pugin to Edward James Wilson, 17 July 1835, in Belcher, M (ed) 2001 *The Collected Letters of A W N Pugin*, **1**. Oxford: Oxford University Press, 48.

2 Pugin to Wilson, 16 August 1835, in Belcher *Collected Letters* **1**, 49.

3 Wedgwood, A 1994 'Domestic Architecture' in Atterbury, P and Wainwright, C (eds) *Pugin: A Gothic Passion*. London: Yale, 45.

4 Wedgwood 'Domestic Architecture', 45.

5 Piper, J 1945 'St Marie's Grange: The First Home of A W N Pugin'. *Architectural Review* **98**, 91.

6 Pugin, A W N 1843 *The Present State of Ecclesiastical Architecture in England*. London: Charles Dolman, 98.

7 Pugin, A W N 1843 *An Apology for the Revival of Christian Architecture in England*. London: John Weale, 4.

8 Powell, C 2006 *Augustus Welby Pugin, Designer of the Houses of Parliament: The Victorian Quest for a Liturgical Architecture*. Lewiston, NY: Edwin Mellen, 67.

9 Belcher, M (ed) 2015 *The Collected Letters of A W N Pugin*, **5**. Oxford: Oxford University Press, xii.

10 Wedgwood 'Domestic Architecture', 57.

11 Bishop Walsh, while addressed with the title 'Bishop' from the time of his first appointment, was not technically a bishop until the hierarchy was reestablished in 1852.

12 Pugin *Present State*, 102.

13 Ibid, 99.

14 Ibid, 100.

15 Ibid, 99.

16 Tim Brittain-Catlin has brought an architect's eye to understanding the centrality of circulation space to architectural effect in Pugin's work, and this analysis of the role of corridors at the Bishop's House is taken from his work. Brittain-Catlin, T 2008 *The English Parsonage in the Early Nineteenth Century*. Reading: Spire, 138–43.

17 Girouard, M 1971 *The Victorian Country House*. Oxford: Clarendon, 44.

18 For the Grange wallpaper, see Stanford, C 2008 *The Grange, Ramsgate*. Maidenhead: The Landmark Trust, 33.

19 Paul Atterbury's essay, 'Pugin and interior design' gives excellent insight into Pugin's work as a decorator and is essential for those who wish to understand his residential work *in toto*. Atterbury, P 1995 'Pugin and interior design' in Atterbury, P (ed) *A W N Pugin: Master of Gothic Revival*. London: Yale.

20 Atterbury 'Pugin and interior design', 180.

21 Girouard *The Victorian Country House*, 113–14.

22 Atterbury 'Pugin and interior design', 179–80.

23 Pugin, A W N 1841 *The True Principles of Pointed or Christian Architecture*. London: John Weale (facsim edn Spire 2003), 40–2.

24 Stansky, P 1996 *Redesigning the World: William Morris, the 1880s, and the Arts and Crafts*. Palo Alto: Society for the Promotion of Science and Scholarship, 48.

25 Atterbury 'Pugin and interior design', 195.

26 Wedgwood, A (ed) 1988? '*Pugin in His Home*': A Memoir by J H Powell. Ramsgate: Pugin Society, 10.

27 Ibid, 11–12.

28 Ibid, 11.

29 Pugin to Bloxam, 26 September 1843, in Belcher, M (ed) 2003 *The Collected Letters of A W N Pugin* 2. Oxford: Oxford University Press, 110.

30 Pugin *True Principles*, 58.

31 Ibid, 59.

32 Wedgwood 'Domestic Architecture', 56.

33 Stanford *The Grange, Ramsgate*, 31.

34 Belcher *Collected Letters* 1, 52.

35 Rosemary Hill's work most compellingly explores this concept: Hill, R 2007 *God's Architect: Pugin and the Building of Romantic Britain*. London: Penguin.

36 Pugin *True Principles*, 61.

37 Timothy Brittain-Caitlin told the author about the pinwheel motif. Notes in author's possession.

38 Stanford *The Grange, Ramsgate*, 27.

39 Hill *God's Architect*, 293.

40 Pugin to Bloxam, 26 September 1843?, in Belcher *Collected Letters* 2, 110 and Pugin to Shrewsbury, 23 June 1847, in Belcher, M (ed) 2009 *The Collected Letters of A W N Pugin* 3. Oxford: Oxford University Press, 246.

3 The seat of wisdom

1 Jesus College website. jesus.cam.ac.uk [accessed 10 October 2018].

2 Pugin, A W N 1841 *Contrasts: Or a Parallel Between the Noble Edifices of the Middle Ages and Corresponding Buildings of the Present Day: Shewing the Present Decay of Taste*. London: Charles Dolman (facsim edn Spire 2003).

3 Pugin, A W N 1843 *The Present State of Ecclesiastical Architecture in England*. London: Charles Dolman, 93.

4 For an insightful study of Pugin's idea of propriety in an anthropological context, see Blundell-Jones, P 2006 'A W N Pugin's Concept of "Propriety" – And What Might Lie Behind It'. *True Principles* 3:3, 6. Pugin, A W N 1841 *The True Principles of Pointed or Christian Architecture*. London: John Weale (facsim edn Spire 2003), iii:iii, 10.

5 Pugin *True Principles*, 42.

6 Stanton, P 1971 *Pugin*. New York: Viking, 52.

7   O'Donnell, R 1995 'The Pugins in Ireland' in Atterbury, P (ed) 1995 A W N Pugin: Master of Gothic Revival. London: Yale, 148.

8   Pugin True Principles, 51.

9   Now known as University College, London. Pugin True Principles, 54.

10 Pugin True Principles, 54.

11 Pugin, A W N 1843 An Apology for the Revival of Christian Architecture in England. London: John Weale, 3 n.

12 Ibid.

13 The architectural changes encouraged by the Oxford Movement and the way a battle for the soul of Britain's churches raged in Oxford is best explored in William Whyte 2017 Unlocking the Church: The Lost Secrets of Victorian Sacred Space. Oxford: Oxford University Press.

14 Hill, R 2007 God's Architect: Pugin & the Building of Romantic Britain. London: Penguin, 204–5.

15 Pugin's 'gin-palace' quotation is in Apology, 3.

16 Colvin, H 1983 Unbuilt Oxford. London: Yale, 113 and 120.

17 For a detailed retelling of the story of Pugin's work at Balliol, see Colvin Unbuilt Oxford, 105–12.

18 Balliol College Archives website, archives.balliol.ox.ac.uk [accessed 10 October 2018].

19 A History of the County of Oxford: vol 3. Victoria County History, London, 1954, 82–95, online at British History Online. www.british-history.ac.uk/vch/oxon/vol3/pp82-95 [accessed 24 September 2018].

20 Pugin to Bloxam, 29 September 1843, Belcher, M (ed) 2003 The Collected Letters of A W N Pugin 2. Oxford: Oxford University Press, 113.

21 Jesus College website.

22 Royal Commission on the Historical Monuments of England 1988 An Inventory of the Historical Monuments in the City of Cambridge 1. London: Stationery Office, 87.

23 These statistics, and those about the orders for which Pugin built, come from Hyland, G J 2014 The Architectural Works of A W N Pugin: A Catalogue. Reading: Spire, 111. Of Pugin's two monasteries, the design for the Presentation Brothers in Ireland is not firmly attributed.

24 The theory that Pugin learned this approach to design by studying his print collection comes from Stanton, 155–163.

25 Pugin Present State, 90.

26 Ibid, 92.

27 Quoted in Hyland Architectural Works, 111–12.

28 Ibid, 112.

29 Stanton Pugin, 189.

30 Hill God's Architect, 215.

31 Ibid, 216.

4 The golden throne

1   Pugin, A W N 1843 An Apology for the Revival of Christian Architecture in England. London: John Weale, 10.

2   Port, M H (ed) 1976 The Houses of Parliament. London: Yale, 94.

3   Ibid.

4   Many scholars believe that the profile of Big Ben was inspired by Pugin's designs for Scarisbrick Hall. This claim seems to be based on the clocktower in the 1836 drawings for Parliament, which shares similarities with Pugin's contemporaneous work at Scarisbrick. However, the extent of Pugin's involvement in designing the Parliament clocktower is merely speculative. Port The Houses of Parliament, 159.

5 See Gillin, E J 2017 *The Victorian Palace of Science: Scientific Knowledge and the Building of the Houses of Parliament*. Cambridge: Cambridge University Press.

6 Collins, M 2012 Talk at V&A Pugin study day. Notes in author's possession.

7 Quoted in Wedgwood, A 1994 'The new Palace of Westminster' in Atterbury, P and Wainwright, C (eds) 1994 *Pugin: A Gothic Passion*. London: Yale, 219.

8 The story of the competition is told in detail in Port, MH (ed) 1976 *The Houses of Parliament*. London: Yale.

9 Pugin's letter setting out his terms appears to have been written on 8 February 1845, and is transcribed from the original and annotated in Belcher, M and Wedgwood, A 2018 'Letters from Pugin to Charles Barry'. *True Principles* **5**:3, 140–1. The version in Margaret Belcher (ed) 2003 *The Collected Letters of A W N Pugin* **2** (Oxford: Oxford University Press) was transcribed from the version printed by Alfred Barry and contains minor discrepancies.

10 Port *The Houses of Parliament*.

11 Some idea of what he might have done can be gleaned from Gillespie Graham's entry in the Parliament competition, in which Pugin is presumed to have had a greater hand. Port *The Houses of Parliament*.

12 Belcher and Wedgwood 'Letters from Pugin to Charles Barry', 134–6.

13 Ibid, inside cover.

14 Pugin *Apology*, 31.

15 Ibid, 38.

16 Wedgwood, A (ed) 1988? '*Pugin in His Home': A Memoir by J H Powell*. Ramsgate: Pugin Society, 16.

17 Pugin, A W N 1838 'Ancient style of family portraits'. *The London and Dublin Orthodox Journal of Useful Knowledge*, 14 July 1838, **VII**:159, 17–18.

18 Pugin *Apology*, 43.

19 Ibid, 43–4.

20 Ibid, 43.

21 Pugin to Barry, 7 June 1845, Belcher and Wedgwood 'Letters from Pugin to Charles Barry', 143.

22 Wainwright, C 1995 'A W N Pugin and the progress of design as applied to manufacture' in Atterbury, P (ed) *A W N Pugin: Master of Gothic Revival*. London: Yale, 164.

23 Pugin *Apology*, 21.

24 For a discussion of Pugin and architectural history, see Levine, N 2010 *Modern Architecture: Representation and Reality*. New Haven: Yale, 118.

25 She would later go on to commission the Albert Memorial.

26 Giles Gilbert Scott, Sketchbook, *c* 1905, Giles Gilbert Scott Papers, RIBA, SKB/302/2.

27 Pugin, A W N 1841 *The True Principles of Pointed or Christian Architecture*. London: John Weale (facsim edn Spire 2003), 40–2.

28 Hill, R 2007 *God's Architect: Pugin and the Building of Romantic Britain*. London: Penguin, 221.

29 Pugin, A W N 1843 *The Present State of Ecclesiastical Architecture in England*. London: Charles Dolman, 152–3.

30 Pugin *Apology*, 39.

31 Wainwright 'A W N Pugin and the progress of design as applied to manufacture'.

32 Pugin *Apology*, 18.

33 This discussion of Pugin and manufacturing is indebted to Wainwright, C 1995 'AWN Pugin and the progress of design as applied to manufacture' in Atterbury, P et al 1995 *A W N Pugin: Master of Gothic Revival*. London: Yale, 173–4.

34 Pugin *Apology*, 8.

35 Belcher, M (ed) 2015 *The Collected Letters of A W N Pugin* **5**. Oxford: Oxford University Press, n4. See also Stanton, P 1971 *Pugin*. New York: Viking, 205.

36 Pugin *Apology*, 5.

37 Pugin to Barry, 5 August 1845, Belcher and Wedgwood 2018 'Letters from Pugin to Charles Barry', 146–7.

5 En avant

1 Nicholson, C and Spooner, C 1910 *Recent Ecclesiastical Architecture*. London: Technical Journals, 3.

2 Marriott, C 1924 *Modern English Architecture*. London: Chapman & Hall, 64.

3 Hill, R 2007 *God's Architect: Pugin and the Building of Romantic Britain*. London: Penguin, 3–4, points to Pevsner's legacy in the interpretation of Pugin.

4 Stanton, P 1971 *Pugin*. New York: Viking.

List of works

Pugin was an enormously prolific designer. The list here contains works mentioned in the text. A complete catalogue of his known works has been compiled by G J Hyland and published as *The Architectural Works of A W N Pugin*, Salisbury: Spire, 2014.

1835: Salisbury, Wiltshire – St Marie's Grange

1835–77: Westminster, London – Houses of Parliament

1837–40: Oscott (now Birmingham), West Midlands – St Mary's College (decorated chapel etc)

1837–40: Reading, Berkshire – St James's

1837–41: Kenmore, Perth & Kinross – Taymouth Castle (decoration)

1837–45: Scarisbrick, Lancashire – Scarisbrick Hall

1837–52: Alton, Staffordshire – The Towers (additions and renovations)

1838–9: Bree, County Wexford – Church of the Assumption

1838–9: Derby, Derbyshire – St Mary's

1838–9: Uttoxeter, Staffordshire – St Mary's

1838–40: Wexford, County Wexford – St Peter's College (decorated chapel)

1838–44: Bermondsey, London – Convent for Sisters of Mercy

1839–41: Macclesfield, Cheshire – St Alban's

1839–41: Birmingham, West Midlands – St Chad's (now cathedral)

1839–43: Gorey, County Wexford – St Michael's

1840–1: Birmingham, West Midlands – Bishop's House

1840–4: Coalville, Leicestershire – Mount St Bernard Priory

1840–50: Handsworth, Birmingham, West Midlands – Convent for Sisters of Mercy

1840–56: Alton, Staffordshire – Hospital of St John the Baptist

1841–2: Stockton-on-Tees, County Durham – St Mary's

1841–8: Southwark, London – St George's (now cathedral)

1842–4: Nottingham, Nottinghamshire – St Barnabas' (now cathedral)

1842–4: Newcastle-upon-Tyne, Tyne & Wear – Our Lady of the Assumption (now cathedral)

1842–6: Cheadle, Staffordshire – St Giles'

1842–8: Waterford, County Waterford
– Convent for the Presentation
Sisters

1842–55: Killarney, County Kerry – St
Mary's (cathedral)

1843–4: Oxford, Oxfordshire –
Magdalen College gateway

1843–5: Ramsgate, Kent – The
Grange

1843–6: Tagoat, County Wexford – St
Mary's

1843–52: Alton, Staffordshire – Alton
Castle (reconstruction)

1843–73: Enniscorthy, County
Wexford – St Aidan's (cathedral)

1844–5: Liverpool, Merseyside – St
Marie

1844–7: Liverpool, Merseyside
– Oswaldcroft

1844–8: Durham, County Durham –
Ushaw College chapel (demolished
and rebuilt)

1844–51: Barnstown, County
Wexford – St Alphonsus'

1844–51: Dunchurch, Warwickshire
– Bilton Grange (additions and
renovations)

1845 (?): Midleton, County Cork
– townhouses

1845–8: Great Marlow,
Buckinghamshire – St Peter's

1845–8: Rampisham, Dorset
– Rectory

1846–52: Cambridge,
Cambridgeshire – Jesus College
chapel (restoration)

1847: Rugby, Warwickshire – St
Marie's

1847–8: Salisbury, Wiltshire – St
Osmund's

1847–50: Maynooth, County Kildare
– St Patrick's College

1847–50: Ramsgate, Kent – St
Augustine's

1850–1: Oatlands, Tasmania – St
Paul's

1850–2: Bicton, Devon – Rolle Family
Chapel

1851: Lismore, County Waterford –
Lismore Castle (redecoration)

Bibliography

Alexander, M 2007 *Medievalism: The Middle Ages in Modern England*. London: Yale

Andrews, B 1994 'Pugin in Australia' in Atterbury, P and Wainwright, C (eds) 1994 *Pugin: A Gothic Passion*. London: Yale, 246–57

Andrews, B 2002 *Creating a Gothic Paradise: Pugin at the Antipodes*. Hobart: Tasmanian Museum and Art Gallery

Anon 1848 *Description of the College Chapel of St Cuthbert, Ushaw*

Atterbury, P 1995 'Pugin and interior design' in Atterbury, P (ed) *A W N Pugin: Master of Gothic Revival*. London: Yale, 177–99

Atterbury, P (ed) 1995 *A W N Pugin: Master of Gothic Revival*. London: Yale

Atterbury, P and Wainwright, C (eds) 1994 *Pugin: A Gothic Passion*. London: Yale

Basciano J 2016 'Notre-Dame de Bonsecours (1840–1844) and the Catholic context of the French Gothic Revival' in Brittain-Catlin, T, DeMeyer, J, and Bressani, M (eds) *Gothic Revival Worldwide: A W N Pugin's Global Influence*. Leuven: Leuven Univ, KADOC-Artes, 32–41

Belcher, M 1987 *A W N Pugin: An Annotated Critical Bibliography*. London: Mansell

Belcher, M (ed) 2001 *The Collected Letters of A W N Pugin 1: 1830–1842*. Oxford: Oxford University Press

Belcher, M (ed) 2003 *The Collected Letters of A W N Pugin 2: 1843–1845*. Oxford: Oxford University Press

Belcher, M (ed) 2009 *The Collected Letters of A W N Pugin 3: 1846–1848*. Oxford: Oxford University Press

Belcher, M (ed) 2012 *The Collected Letters of A W N Pugin 4: 1849–1850*. Oxford: Oxford University Press

Belcher, M (ed) 2015 *The Collected Letters of A W N Pugin 5: 1851–1852*. Oxford: Oxford University Press

Belcher, M and Wedgwood, A 2018 'Letters from Pugin to Charles Barry'. *True Principles* **5**:3

Betjeman, J 2014 *Lovely Bits of Old England: Selected Writings from* The Telegraph. London: Aurum

Blundell-Jones, P 2006 'A W N Pugin's concept of "propriety" – and what might lie behind it'. *True Principles* **3**:3

Bremner, A (ed) 2012 *Ecclesiology Abroad: The British Empire and Beyond.* Studies in Victorian Architecture & Design 4. London: Victorian Society

Brittain-Catlin, T 2008 *The English Parsonage in the Early Nineteenth Century.* Reading: Spire

Brittain-Catlin, T, DeMeyer, J, and Bressani, M (eds) 2016 *Gothic Revival Worldwide: A W N Pugin's Global Influence.* Leuven: Leuven Univ, KADOC-Artes 16

Coffman, P 2016 'Meanings of Gothic in Atlantic Canada: c 1840–1890' in Brittain-Catlin, T, DeMeyer, J, and Bressani, M (eds) *Gothic Revival Worldwide: A W N Pugin's Global Influence.* Leuven: Leuven Univ, KADOC-Artes, 64–75

Colvin, H 1983 *Unbuilt Oxford.* London: Yale

Fisher, M 2012 *'Gothic for Ever': A W N Pugin, Lord Shrewsbury, and the Rebuilding of Catholic England.* Reading: Spire

Fisher, M 2013 *St Giles Church, Cheadle.* Stoke-on-Trent: Urban Vision

Gillin, E J 2017 *The Victorian Palace of Science: Scientific Knowledge and the Building of the Houses of Parliament.* Cambridge: Cambridge University Press

Girouard, M 1971 *The Victorian Country House.* Oxford: Clarendon

Hill, R 2007 *God's Architect: Pugin and the Building of Romantic Britain.* London: Penguin

Horner, L and Hunter, G 2000 *A Flint Seaside Church: St Augustine's Abbey Church, Ramsgate.* Ramsgate: Pugin Society

Hyland, G J 2014 *The Architectural Works of A W N Pugin: A Catalogue.* Reading: Spire

Hyland, G J 2018 *Beyond 'Puginism'.* Reading: Spire

Lesser, W 2017 *You Say to Brick: The Life of Louis Kahn.* New York: Farrar, Straus and Giroux

Levine, N 2010 *Modern Architecture: Representation and Reality.* New Haven: Yale

McNair, S 2016 'Richard Upjohn and the Gothic in Antebellum Alabama' in Brittain-Catlin, T, DeMeyer, J, and Bressani, M (eds) *Gothic Revival Worldwide: A W N Pugin's Global Influence.* Leuven: Leuven Univ, KADOC-Artes, 106–17

Marriott, C 1924 *Modern English Architecture.* London: Chapman & Hall

Nicholson, C and Spooner, C 1907 *Recent Ecclesiastical Architecture.* London: Technical Journals

O'Donnell, R 1994 'Pugin as church architect' in Atterbury, P and Wainwright, C (eds) *Pugin: A Gothic Passion.* London: Yale, 62–89

O'Donnell, R 1995 'The Pugins in Ireland' in Atterbury, P (ed) 1995 *A W N Pugin: Master of Gothic Revival.* London: Yale, 137–60

O'Donnell, R 2002 *Pugin and the Catholic Midlands.* Leominster: Gracewing

Piper, J 1945 'St Marie's Grange: The First Home of A W N Pugin'. *Architectural Review* 98, 90–93

Port, M H (ed) 1976 *The Houses of Parliament*. London: Yale

Powell, C 2006 *Augustus Welby Pugin, Designer of the Houses of Parliament: The Victorian Quest for a Liturgical Architecture*. Lewiston, NY: Edwin Mellen

Pugin, A C 1821–c 1825 *Specimens of Gothic Architecture*. London: J Taylor

Pugin, A C 1838–40 *Examples of Gothic Architecture*. London: Henry Bohn

Pugin, A W N 1838 'Ancient style of family portraits'. *The London and Dublin Orthodox Journal of Useful Knowledge*, 14 July 1838, VII:159

Pugin, A W N 1838 'Lectures on ecclesiastical architecture: Lecture the First' reprinted in *True Principles* **5**:2, 84–105

Pugin, A W N 1841 *Contrasts: Or a Parallel Between the Noble Edifices of the Middle Ages and Corresponding Buildings of the Present Day: Shewing the Present Decay of Taste*. London: Charles Dolman (facsim edn Spire 2003)

Pugin, A W N 1841 *The True Principles of Pointed or Christian Architecture*. London: John Weale (facsim edn Spire 2003)

Pugin, A W N 1843 *An Apology for the Revival of Christian Architecture in England*. London: John Weale

Pugin, A W N 1843 *The Present State of Ecclesiastical Architecture in England*. London: Charles Dolman

Pugin, A W N 1844 *Glossary of Ecclesiastical Ornament and Costume*. London: Henry Bohn

Pugin, A W N 1849 *Floriated Ornament*. London: Henry Bohn

Pugin Society 1990s–present *True Principles: The Journal of the Pugin Society*, 1–5

Richardson, D S 1970 *Gothic Revival Architecture in Ireland*. PhD dissertation, Yale University

Royal Commission on the Historical Monuments of England 1988 *An Inventory of the Historical Monuments in the City of Cambridge 1*. London: Stationery Office

Saint, A 2005 'St Chad's, Birmingham: Not so very foreign?' *True Principles* **3**:2, 70

Shepherd, S 2009 *Stained Glass of A W N Pugin*. Reading: Spire

Stamp, G 2015 *Gothic for the Steam Age*. London: Aurum

Stanford, C 2004 *Dearest Augustus and I*. Reading: Spire

Stanford, C 2008 *The Grange, Ramsgate*. Maidenhead: The Landmark Trust

Stansky, P 1996 *Redesigning the World: William Morris, the 1880s, and the Arts and Crafts*. Palo Alto: Society for the Promotion of Science and Scholarship

Stanton, P 1971 *Pugin*. New York: Viking

Trappes-Lomax, M 1932 *Pugin: A Medieval Victorian*. London: Sheed & Ward

Wainwright, C 1995 'A W N Pugin and the progress of design as applied to manufacture' in Atterbury, P (ed) *A W N Pugin: Master of Gothic Revival*. London: Yale, 161–75

Watkin, D 1977 *Morality and Architecture*. Chicago: Chicago University Press

Webster, J 2011 'A W N Pugin's Grange at Ramsgate'. *True Principles* **4**:2, 191–2

Wedgwood, A 1985 *A W N Pugin and the Pugin Family*. London: Victoria and Albert Museum

Wedgwood, A (ed) 1988? *'Pugin in His Home': A Memoir by J H Powell*. Ramsgate: Pugin Society

Wedgwood, A 1994 'Domestic Architecture' in Atterbury, P and Wainwright, C (eds) *Pugin: A Gothic Passion*. London: Yale, 43–61

Wedgwood, A 1994 'The New Palace of Westminster' in Atterbury, P and Wainwright, C (eds) *Pugin: A Gothic Passion*. London: Yale, 219–36

Whyte, W 2017 *Unlocking the Church: The Lost Secrets of Victorian Sacred Space*. Oxford: Oxford University Press

Index